Regardless of Frontiers
Children's rights and global learning

WITHDRAWN

Regardless of Frontiers
Children's rights and global learning

Don Harrison

Trentham Books

Stoke on Trent, UK and Sterling, USA

Trentham Books Limited
Westview House   22883 Quicksilver Drive
734 London Road   Sterling
Oakhill   VA 20166-2012
Stoke on Trent   USA
Staffordshire
England ST4 5NP

First published 2008

British Library Cataloguing-in-Publication Data
A catalogue record for this book is available from the British Library

ISBN: 978 1 85856 400 5

Cover image: Panama – Children of different countries learning together.

The Material on pages 16 and 19 is reproduced from *Deadlines: Media bias about
the Third World - A simulation for secondary schools (1984)/ TILT NINE* (1985) with
the permission of Oxfam GB, Oxfam House, John Smith Drive, Cowley, Oxford OX4
2JY, UK www.oxfam.org.uk/education. Oxfam GB does not necessarily endorse any
text or activities that accompany the materials.'

Designed and typeset by Trentham Print Design Ltd, Chester and printed
in Great Britain by Hobbs the Printers, Hampshire.

Contents

Acknowledgements

This book is dedicated to the children whose lives I have been privileged to share in Burkina Faso, England, Malawi, Malaysia, Panama, Peru, Scotland and Somalia. Some of their words and pictures are presented here, acknowledging a trusted copyright put in my hands to further their rights to expression. Most will now be adults and will be pleased to know that their visions may be helping teachers and other school pupils to learn about their worlds of childhood.

Fieldwork examples from projects with children come mostly from Save the Children's development education unit which has inspired a lot of the thinking and practice in this book. Many thanks are due to Andrew Hutchinson for his vision that Global Child Rights Education is both possible and valuable. Thanks also for project work from the City Academy in Bristol.

Introduction

A s the title suggests, this book is about children sharing ideas across frontiers of any kind, as required by Article 13.1 of the UN *Convention on the Rights of the Child*

> The child shall have the right to freedom of expression; this right shall include freedom to seek, receive and impart information and ideas of all kinds, regardless of frontiers, either orally, in writing or in print, in the form of art, or through any other media of the child's choice.

Chapter 1 introduces the UN *Convention* as an important educational document although not all teachers may be familiar with it. It relates the *Convention* to other visions for improving children's lives, including the UK's *Every Child Matters*.

Chapter 2 separates learning *through* rights and learning *about* rights. Each is shown in fieldwork sections based on my experience as an English teacher and NGO education worker.

I began my career as a pre-university English teacher in Malawi and, after qualifying as an English teacher, in Cameroon and Yorkshire. During the early 1980s I worked for Oxfam as a regional education adviser. From this phase I have chosen examples of *learning rights*: expression, information and respect as groundwork for envisioning learning across frontiers.

After teaching English in Malaysia during the later 1980s, I worked for Save the Children's Education unit, creating materials and training teachers. Recently I have worked for Citizenship NGOs and as an English teacher for refugees in Bristol. From this phase I have chosen examples and children's drawings of *welfare rights,* to give a global rights dimension to the five outcomes of *Every Child Matters.*

Chapter 3 offers practical advice for teachers, based on my previous practice and my later career. Returning to Save the Children's education unit from 2004 to 2005 and then as a lecturer for humans rights education at Bath Spa University, I have had opportunities to clarify my thinking about a coherent model for teaching children's rights.

The last chapters give more practical information about activities and resources that I recommend for teachers who wish to develop their pupils' learning about rights with a global dimension.

My hope is that readers of this book will be inspired to help make children's own realities a more visible and vocal source of learning about children. As T S Eliot wrote in his poem *Burnt Norton*

> Go, said the bird, for the leaves were full of children,
> Hidden excitedly, containing laughter.
> Go, go, go, said the bird: human kind
> Cannot bear very much reality.

1
Children's rights

This section introduces the 1989 UN *Convention on the Rights of the Child* (from here simply called the *Convention*). It stresses the educational dimensions of the *Convention* for rights and responsibilities and relates them to other important documents: *Every Child Matters*, the Millennium Development Goals and the UK Human Rights Act.

The Convention on the Rights of the Child

States Parties undertake to make the principles and provisions of the Convention widely known, by appropriate and active means, to adults and children alike. Article 42

Children's rights are the human rights all children should have. Universally accepted values are still evolving, so as the twenty-first century progresses children's rights will be seen differently. Like all rights, there are reciprocal responsibilities.

All children are entitled to special rights on account of being young. This is a comparatively recent development. The notion of childhood as distinct from adulthood evolved over the twentieth century, inspired by visionary books such as Aries' *Centuries of Childhood* to Cunningham's *The Invention of Childhood* (Cunningham, 2006; Osler and Starkey, 2005).

The history of children's rights can be dated from 1924, when English philanthropist Eglantyne Jebb presented five points to the League of Nations in Geneva. The League adopted them and proclaimed the first ever international *Declaration of the Rights of the Child*, also known as the *Declaration of Geneva*. With her sister Dorothy Buxton, Eglantyne Jebb founded the Save the Children Fund and she devoted her short life to the welfare of the world's children.

The understanding of children's rights has developed over time. This is apparent when we compare the language and concepts of the 1924 *Declaration* with the 1989 *Convention on the Rights of the Child*. The Geneva Declaration stated:

- The child must be given the means for its normal development both materially and spiritually

- The child that is hungry must be fed; the child that is sick must be nursed; the child that is backward must be helped; the delinquent child must be reclaimed; and the orphan and the waif must be sheltered and succoured

- The child must be first to receive relief in times of distress

- The child must be put in a position to earn a livelihood and must be protected against every form of exploitation

- The child must be brought up in the consciousness that its talents must be devoted to the service of its fellow men
(Quoted in Save the Children's *Changing Childhoods* 1996: 66)

This 1924 *Declaration* was an idealistic statement of principles to guide the way adult societies should care for their children. After the collapse of the League of Nations and the descent into a world war that brutalised children's lives, the new United Nations made a renewed attempt to take an idealistic approach to children. It revived and expanded Jebb's original points into a ten point *Declaration of the Rights of the Child* in 1959 and created the *International Year of the Child* in 1979. This led to the setting up of a working group to consider the government of Poland's proposal for a stronger and more official convention for children's rights. After ten more years of consultation, which to a limited extent involved children, the new convention was drafted and presented to the UN General Assembly on 20 November 1989. This date is now International Children's Day.

The 1989 *Convention on the Rights of the Child* is the key document now in place. It is in three parts. The first lays down 42 rights for all children up to the age of eighteen. The second and third parts are about the implementation of these rights. A UN Committee on the Rights of the Child is empowered to review the progress of governments that have ratified the *Convention*. By 2006 every independent nation state in the world, bar the USA and Somalia, had signed up to what has become the most widely accepted international document of all time. The UK Government ratified the *Convention* in 1991 with a few reservations and has to some extent incorporated its provisions into its policies for children as in the values enshrined in the policy document of 2004, *Every Child Matters*.

The 42 new rights for children represent a large expansion on the League's original five points, particularly in regard to children's participation in society. There are many ways of viewing and summarising what the *Convention* offers children. Amnesty International, Plan International, Save the Children, UNICEF and other non-government organisations (NGOs) produce child-friendly posters and leaflets that outline the *Convention*. The newly clarified rights for children cover provision, protection and participation.

Provision rights include: survival and development (Article 6), health care (Article 24), adequate standard of living (Article 27), education (Articles 28 and 29) and play and leisure (Article 30).

Protection rights include: protection from abuse and neglect (Article 19), being without a family (Article 20), being a refugee (Article 22), and against child labour (Article 32), drug abuse (Article 33), sexual exploitation (Article 34), torture, and armed conflicts (Articles 37 and 38).

Participation rights include: holding and expressing opinions (Articles 12 and 13), association (Article 15) and information (Article 17) as well as the social and cultural rights of minorities and indigenous peoples (Article 30).

As this brief summary indicates, there is no particular rational order in the *Convention*. The structure closely follows the arrangement of rights in the 1948 *Universal Declaration of Human Rights*. Underlying the provision, protection and participation rights are the unequivocal statements in the opening Articles of the *Convention* that the rights apply to all children and young people on a basis of equality and non-discrimination (Article 2) and that the 'best interests of the child' should be paramount (Article 3).

All the rights in the *Convention* apply to 'every human being below the age of eighteen years unless, under the law applicable to the child, majority is attained earlier' (from Article One). The rights apply to all children 'without discrimination of any kind' (from Article Two). This has raised philosophical questions about who exactly can be called a child. Priscilla Alderson, among others, has developed understanding of the rights of the youngest children (Alderson, 2000) and more recently of premature babies. The rights of unborn children were an issue of contested debate during the drawing up of the *Convention*.

In a recent book on child rights legislation around the world, Michael Freeman wrote about the need to revise the *Convention* in the light of the rights of special groups of children that were not specifically acknowledged in 1989, including 'children with HIV/AIDS, street children, child soldiers, the gay child, the indigenous child' (Freeman, 2004, II 289). Freeman's view is that these are problems which were not seen as significant then and are 'better grappled with today'. This gives an additional perspective for seeing the value for teaching and learning based on the *Convention*. It is the most universally agreed statement to date of all the entitlement to rights of all the world's children.

The *Convention* relates to educational policy in general as well as to schooling and curriculum provision. Awareness of the *Convention* itself is crucial. Teachers have to know what is provided for in its education rights and the implications for strengthening children's participation in society as young citizens.

Governments that ratify the *Convention* are signing up to Article 42 to make the *Convention* widely known. The UK Government has yet to put this Article to full effect, although there are recent moves in the Ministry of Justice to increase funding and support for awareness of human rights. Many countries have greater public awareness than the UK and a growing culture of children's rights, as evident from posters in public places. The non-government organisation materials and projects featured in this book could certainly be more widely used in the UK and official summary statements and visual support material need to be made available. Article 42 provides for active means of learning and underlines the importance of making adults as well as children aware of the rights all children should have.

Children's responsibilities

The child must be brought up in the consciousness that its talents must be devoted to the service of its fellow men. (*Declaration of Geneva* 1924, point 5)

The language of public service is beginning to re-surface in the UK. There are ideas for national service schemes and Community Service Volunteers advertise regularly for people to help with local community development projects. Citizens in the UK may have lost the sense of social cohesion they once felt they had. People lead more individualised or techno-dominated lives and affluence has increased. A comparison of lifestyles in Scotland and Panama (see section 2.2) highlights the way European children risk losing a community focus, whereas children elsewhere are more likely to relate closely to adults with whom they do things together as they always have.

Eglantyne Jebb's original vision for children's rights included the right to grow up with a spirit of service to others. Philosophies of rights emphasise that the giving of rights implies the recognition of reciprocal duties (Freeman, 2002). Rights imply responsibilities, although some people find the *Convention* very strong on rights but less forceful about telling children about their social responsibilities. The National Curriculum for Citizenship in England focuses on responsibilities more than rights. The way forward must be to reconcile the two concepts so that young people are guided towards a balanced view of how they relate to each other.

Teachers may be concerned that pupils who express strong opinions about their own rights may be less caring about those of others. Emphasising *our* rights rather than *my* rights can foster a global approach. Teachers should give importance to understanding rights but should always link rights to their reciprocal responsibilities. The *Convention* only uses the word responsible in Article 29, in the phrase 'responsible life in a free society', where it competes with many other areas of social, cultural and environmental learning.

The educational literature draws attention to how responsibilities relate to rights (Osler and Starkey, 2005). The problem is that the match may not be obvious enough for young learners to understand and put into practice. It is easy to match the right to free expression with an acknowledgement that this right should go with a responsibility to respect the free expression of others, but more difficult to guide children towards a sense of the responsibility for the right to freedom from torture and unjust imprisonment.

The Citizenship curriculum is the appropriate context for teaching about human rights. Rights do not come free: they need to be understood as a reciprocal deal. This can be likened to a playground swap, where something is given and something else is given back. Classroom discussion might be triggered by an incident in which a child has acted in an anti-social manner: how do the others feel about it and what do they think should be done? Caring for others can be learned through caring for people with visible needs in the local community. The principle is established at local level that if you expect people to respect your wishes, wants or feelings it is right to respect theirs. These principles underpin rights and responsibilities. Charters announcing the principles agreed by the class can be produced and displayed.

On a more abstract and distant level, rights and responsibilities can be linked in a rights framework. This begins with personal rights such as identity, expression, food, shelter, care and education and extends to a wider range as presented in the *Convention* such as survival, protection and justice for everyone. It includes the rights of special groups like disabled children or children who are refugees and asylum seekers. Teachers can build on pupils' understanding of the value of caring for others to develop their thinking about specific situations. The real life situations of this other group will be remote from their own experience.

As pupils become more aware of rights issues they may be able to take on some of the responsibility for helping children who need it to get their rights. Learning about social responsibilities is an essential component of effective citizenship education and is enhanced by being seen through a prism of rights. Learning about the importance of acting to care for people in an African country who are going hungry is given more value if it is not just seen as something that needs to be done because teachers or the global community say so. It is better to put this kind of learning in a universal framework of the rights which are shared by all children. This approach helps to establish a sense of shared humanity.

The right to adequate nutrition for normal healthy development may seem obvious but pupils need to learn that not every child has enough to eat. They should be encouraged to develop a sense of responsibility towards the children elsewhere whose nutrition is threatened by social, environmental, political or economic factors. This is the beginning of sound learning for global rights and responsibilities, exploring and sharing values. This is much more than an add-on of charitable activity in an after-school club. It involves the kind of education in values that the school, its teachers and its learning activities stand for.

The *Convention* and other relevant documents

For children growing up in the UK today there are two key statements of entitlement: the *Convention on the Rights of the Child* and *Every Child Matters*. Here I outline the wide range of rights for children in the UN *Convention* as they relate to the outcomes of the UK Government's policy for *Every Child Matters*, although this is not always seen as a rights-based document. Nonetheless, it relates directly to areas of rights for children.

The *Convention* rights outlined above can be grouped in many ways

- rights to equality
- rights to family care
- rights to survival and development
- rights to identity and expression
- rights for refugee children
- rights for children with disabilities
- rights to health care and economic security
- rights to education and leisure
- rights to protection from harmful work
- rights to protection from abuse and torture
- rights to rehabilitation
- rights to justice

The UN *Convention* provides for the rights of all children in the world. *Every Child Matters*, a Government Green Paper published in 2003, concerns provision for children in the UK and has been further strengthened by the 2004 *Children Act* and the appointment in 2005 of a Commissioner for Children in England. The other three UK countries already had commissioners.

Every Child Matters defines five outcomes for children. They should:

- be healthy
- stay safe
- enjoy and achieve
- make a positive contribution
- achieve economic well-being

Every Child Matters sets out for teachers the immediate aims for education. Where pupils are learning about the lives of children beyond the UK, the same outcomes should be applied, so helping summarise the wider range of rights in the *Convention*. The next chapter provides visual evidence from children in five countries to illustrate the importance of the outcomes for all children everywhere and to relate these to the *Convention*.

Behind these two statements for children lie two statements of entitlement for children and adults. *The Human Rights Act*, which applies to UK citizens, and the *Millennium Development Goals* concerned particularly with people in poorer countries of the world.

The 1998 UK *Human Rights Act* came into law in 2000. It brings the *European Convention on Human Rights* into UK law, providing all citizens with:

- the right to life
- rights to protection from torture and forced labour
- rights to liberty, security and justice

- rights to privacy and family life
- rights to freedom of conscience, expression and assembly
- the right to marry

The *Millennium Development Goals* came out of the UN Millennium Summit in New York in 2000 and are aspirations for the global community. They aim by 2015 to

- eradicate extreme poverty and hunger
- achieve universal primary education
- promote gender equality and empower women
- reduce child mortality
- improve maternal health
- combat HIV/AIDS, malaria and other diseases
- ensure environmental sustainability
- secure a global partnership for development

The UK agreements for children's welfare and their rights as citizens are set within a context of agreements for all children's rights and the well-being of the least well off. They provide a context for learning about, from and with children at local, national and global levels.

Summary – the background to children's rights

All children have responsibilities as global citizens. Teachers can help them to understand this through the intersecting fields of education in human rights, citizenship and peace.

The most important of the international statements on children's rights is the 1989 UN *Convention on the Rights of the Child* which the UK Government ratified in 1991. Children's rights provide a universal value base, as codified in the 1989 UN *Convention.*

Awareness of the importance of child rights education is growing in the context of human rights education movements dating from the end of the Second World War or even earlier and the creation of the United Nations. The principles for which I argue, and which inform this book are:

- that children learning their rights should at the same time learn to understand their reciprocal responsibilities

- and that child rights education should be seen in a global context. It is especially important that our pupils learn not from traditional – or adult – constructions, but by listening to what children in various countries themselves say about their experiences of childhood.

2
Global learning

This chapter looks at examples of *learning rights* and *welfare rights* across frontiers. The guidance is drawn from localised examples I have my experienced which will, I hope, be helpful for teachers in a range of subjects and school contexts.

2.1: Learning rights
The right of children to expression

The everyday lives of children can become a visible and aural source for learning across frontiers of nation state, language or culture. Pupils can be helped to explore and express ideas about their world and their values, as shown in the following examples. Exchanging such accounts with pupils in different parts of the world brings authenticity and excitement to the learning process. The rights of children to express their views and ideas are recognised in Articles 12 and 13 of the *Convention*:

> States Parties shall assure to the child who is capable of forming his or her own views the right to express those views freely in all matters affecting the child, the views of the child being given due weight in accordance with the age and maturity of the child. (13.1)

Article 13.1 extends the right to expression to children sharing information and ideas across frontiers. This book shows ways that children's expression can add value to learning about children's rights to achieve in and contribute to society regardless of frontiers. The experiences of children in another country imbue lessons with a global learning dimension.

My first example of the right to expression is drawn from a secondary classroom in the North West Province of Cameroon in the mid 1970s. The school was a purpose built secondary campus on a hillside in the grassland savannah area of the country, formerly the British colony of Southern Cameroons. The pupils were sitting in rows at wooden desks facing a black-painted board. The subject for their writing that day was 'Memories of primary school'.

As a teacher of English I would emphasise to language teachers how important it is to give pupils a positive voice. I found that children's creative work need not just be ticked and returned but can be used for wider communication. During the four years I spent as an Inter-

Being a child from the interior villages of Africa, I thought that school was designed for those who hated hardship and had great love for pleasure. I saw that many of my age-mates were not carrying babies but going to school.

The Miss asked me to sit with a boy and of course this was very strange for I had never sat with a boy before. I refused and stood there till long break. After a month school started to bore me because our teacher was a very wild and hatesome somebody. I thought I was going to paradise, but I was beaten terribly!

Figure 1: Pupil writing from Cameroon (reproduced in SC/UNICEF (1990) The Whole Child).

national Voluntary Service teacher in Cameroon, West Africa during the 1970s, one of the few girls in my English class wrote a short essay on her early memories of schooling (Figure 1). She showed that primary school had not turned out to be the paradise she had imagined when she saw her peers – mainly boys – going there. She was delighted when I promoted her piece of writing with other English teachers. I used it in an article for the *Human Rights Education Newsletter* in 1998, in which I imagined children's voices from around the world responding to the Crick Report on Citizenship. It has also appeared in the 1990 Save the Children and UNICEF topic book *The Whole Child* under the title 'First experiences of school'. The topic of schooling is rich for pupil expression because everyone has something to recall from these early memories. Save the Children recently instigated an exchange of memory books called *Starting School.*

The right of children to information

All children have a right to accurate and beneficial information. This includes learning to understand the hidden messages in certain sources of information. Article 17 of the *Convention* declares:

> States Parties recognise the important function performed by the mass media and shall ensure that the child has access to information and material from a diversity of national and international sources, especially those aimed at the promotion of his or her social, spiritual and moral well-being and physical and mental health.

Consequently, criteria are needed for evaluating how effectively the resources used in schools present children's lives. Films and class materials can be used to help children understand the limitations and bias of the media. The best of the NGO resources emphasise visual images which show children growing up in developing countries in ways that counter the negative light in which they are so often presented.

During my first years as an NGO educator I worked a lot on media images. I was trying to help pupils and teachers see behind stereotypical images of the Third World so they could start to see realities behind the pictures. I helped organise a series of sixth form Media Days at the Africa Centre in London, in collaboration with practising journalists. My second example is set in the main hall of the Africa Centre in the early 1980s. Sixth form students from many schools came together with the support of Oxfam to spend the day learning about how Africa is portrayed in the media.

An imaginary trip was made to Batonga in Africa, where we had to report on a sugar cane crisis in a town that was poverty stricken like many of the third world countries. When we got enough information to satisfy ourselves we returned home to England to inform our fellow Britons of the crisis...

We emphasised the fact that stocks and shares would not be drastically affected; the British were not to worry. However, in the article we did not mention that people were dying as a result of hunger, wages were low and the government was uncontrolled. We failed to report on this as it was not in the interest of our readers...

These articles from the very reliable British newspapers were then read out in turn after completion. Having listened to the same report being distorted and vandalised by different newspapers I felt rather confused, as a disaster so severe could be made to seem so unimportant by the media; naturally readers would believe what was reported.

Figure 2: From a sixth former's evaluation of a 'Media Day', reproduced from Oxfam (1984) Deadlines: Media Bias about the Third World – A simulation for secondary schools.

Each Media Day was built around a simulated disaster scenario. Working in groups, the students covered the fictional disaster as reporters for British newspapers like the *Sun*, the *Daily Telegraph* and the *Morning Star*. This proved an exciting and powerful way of getting home the message that the same story can be given very different slants (Figure 2).

In her history of Oxfam, Maggie Black examines the use of the 'starving baby' images used by NGOs to evoke empathy and charitable giving. She dates this back to the Congo crises of the early 1960s, reinforced later by the Biafran crisis of the late 1960s:

> Gradually, image by image, Oxfam was helping to develop a new way of looking at the world, an ideologically charged view of other countries and cultures, a more considered version of the predicament symbolised by the starving child. It is a great tribute to Oxfam that, in today's Britain, almost no-one's idea of the world beyond Europe and North America is untouched by the perception of humanity in need. (Black, 1992: 104)

Many development NGOs followed this trend. They produced hugely negative images of children intended for classroom use, either indirectly through fundraising activity or directly in their early resources produced for schools. During the 1990s there was a reaction against such overly negative portrayal of children's lives. This was due partly to the global acceptance of the *Convention* and the growing understanding and acceptance that children's privacy and dignity should be respected.

But recently NGOs have again started presenting visual media images that appear to feature negative representations of children. This is possibly because fundraising capacity is shrinking in an era of compassion fatigue, so increasing competition among NGOs for public support. However, within the school sections of these organisations, set up to promote learning about world development, it has been agreed that work in UK schools be based on educational over promotional aims. There have been many collaborative ventures over the years, with resources jointly produced, for example the 1992 poster pack produced by four leading development NGOs for learning about the impact of European discovery of the Americas, and the recent *Get Global!* skills-based resource to help secondary age students enquire about the world.

The right of children to learn respect

Children's actions as young citizens can be shaped by their ability to identify with the daily lives of other children in the world. Their rights to action are part of their entitlement to learn values for a better world and their role in helping to achieve this, both in their own communities and globally. This is the spirit of the *Convention* and is made specific in Article 29 for...

> the preparation of the child for responsible life in a free society, in the spirit of understanding, peace, tolerance, equality of sexes, and friendship among all peoples, ethnic, national and religious groups and persons of indigenous origin. (29.1d)

Article 29c provides for education about pupils' varied cultural backgrounds, including 'the development of respect ... for civilisations different from his or her own'. This is important for teachers who are seeking justification for global learning, especially if the idea of 'civilisations' is taken in the widest possible sense to include all learning about other peoples and communities and not just those deemed historically significant, such as the ancient Egyptians or Romans. Learning about daily life in an African township or Indian village should be presented from the point of view of the local people. Pupils should be learning about the culture of a different civilisation from its own perspective rather than about places which they may see as culturally or economically inferior.

I use the term 'respect' to cover the broad area of values education that includes tolerance and respect for the cultures and lifestyles of people other than ones, own. The third scene I have chosen to illustrate takes place in a middle school classroom in Newcastle, North East England during the mid 1980s. Pupils are involved in a simulated debate between settlers from Java and the indigenous residents of Irian Jaya (Figure 3). They have moved to this 'new island' on a government scheme that offers land. This was at a time when there was international criticism of the Indonesian government because the rights and traditional environments of the Papuan people of Irian Jaya appeared to be under threat from this transmigration scheme.

This is one of a number of drama-based projects I was engaged in while working as an Oxfam education adviser in north east England. I was beginning to see the importance of getting children to use imaginative identification with the lives of other people. I worked with teachers to devise and trial simulation activities and these were written

> ## The Tree People
> We are not being helped because the settlers need money, food, clothes, shoes, rice, land and a house. We wanted the government to stop cutting down our trees and killing our animals but the settlers need land and a house.
>
> ## The settlers
> We have decided to go to the new island because in the city they are very poor and it is far too hot and crowded. And we would not get as much land. They also live in little huts in the city but if we go to the New Island we will get good land and a fine new house.

Figure 3: From TILT NINE on Teaching about Trees (Oxfam, 1985).

up and offered to other teachers in a termly subscription magazine called *TILT*. I also worked with Theatre in Education colleagues to develop an interactive performance drama on the history of a Caribbean island: Rich Port, Poor Port.

Children's experiences can contribute to the creating of role-plays. This makes them seem more realistic because they are closer to the lives of the subjects of the activity. Children can learn imaginatively about global issues affecting children and, as active citizens, plan to do something to effect change.

This section on *learning rights* has been mainly informed by secondary level teaching and NGO projects that ran during the 1970s and 1980s. It offers a foundation for principles of global learning in relation to children's rights. Good practice is about:

- inspiring children to express and share their daily realities. This is particularly effective through learning exchanges between schools in different countries

- promoting children's expressions about their own experience, or to challenge or broaden the often limited or distorted images of children's lives too often presented to pupils in UK schools. This requires pupils to learn about media generally and involves them in making appropriate classroom resources

- devising imaginative ways for pupils to learn about children's lives in different places and circumstances, to complement the enabling of direct expression (see first point) or for use where it is not feasible for those being studied to convey their views and perspectives on their lives by direct expression. Use of dramatic methods like role-play can lead pupils to informed and imaginative action as young citizens

All three of these points are further explored in the classroom experience section in 2.3. What the section above does not cover is the right to education itself, which I see more as a provision right. So access to schooling is considered in the welfare rights section which follows. It describes examples of projects carried out in primary schools.

2.2: Welfare rights

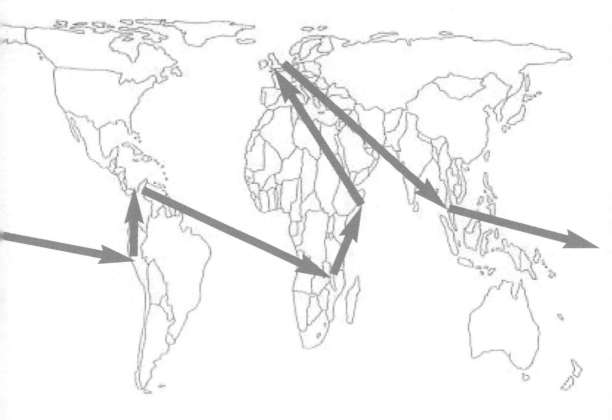

Figure 4: Map of the book's welfare rights studies: from Malaysia to Peru to Panama to Malawi to Somalia to the UK.

The projects described here illustrate ways of learning about children's rights to a decent childhood. Relating the five outcomes in *Every Child Matters* to matching articles in the *Convention* gives them a global focus. I recorded the views of children and these views inform what follows and indicate how teachers can develop their practice in conveying welfare rights to their pupils.

Each section describes a project which has encouraged children to express their views. Their pictures are used to suggest global learning approaches to each of the five outcomes, which I have labelled: security, survival, success, safety and status. The projects are presented in chronological order of their development, but can be used in any order as they are all equally useful for pupils to understand children's rights issues fully.

The right of children to economic security

One of the outcomes of *Every Child Matters* is achieving economic wellbeing. This matches Article 27 of the *Convention* which provides for 'the right of every child to a standard of living adequate for the child's physical, mental, spiritual, moral and social development'. Other relevant Articles include 4 and 5, for the important roles of the family and the state in the life of every child. One of the *Millennium Development Goals* is to reduce hunger and improve family incomes. Although achieving economic well-being is less emphasised in the *Human Rights Act* it does make clear that schools should develop pupils' experience and understanding of poverty issues in the UK and the world.

My fourth illustrative scene is set in a secondary classroom in Kedah State, north west Malaysia during the late 1980s. The pupils are sitting in rows with boys on the left side and girls on the right. Their possessions are in boxes and bags at their feet. The subject of the day's English lesson was their parents' jobs and whether they themselves

Life for the rubber tapper is not easy. I'm sure because my father is a rubber tapper. Before he goes to the rubber farm early in the morning, he only drinks a cup of coffee. He doesn't eat breakfast. It's about 6.30 a.m. he arrives in his farm and starts tapping the rubber trees. He only goes to tap when the weather is good but if it's raining he will not come out.

At 12.30 p.m. he returns home carrying two barrels of rubber liquid on his bicycle. He never takes a nap first but goes straight to the hut where the liquid should be coagulated. The coagulated rubbers are machined into pieces. My father gets only two pieces a day.

He sells them once a month. One kilogramme can bring $1.25. In a month my father only gets about $200. My family consists of 7 people and it is not easy to manage on only $200 per month

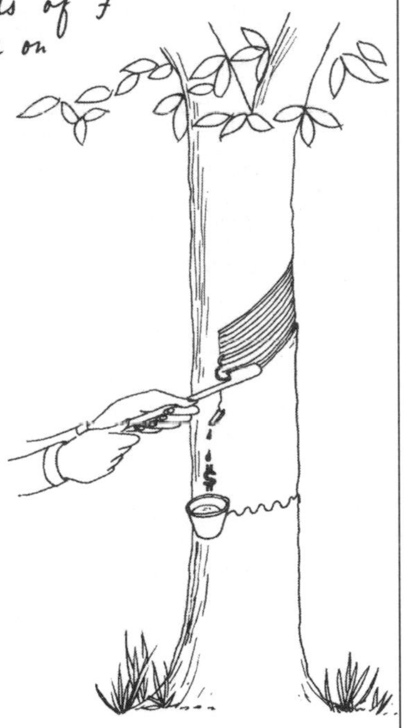

Figure 5: Malaysia – life for the rubber tapper

DIALOUGE BETWEEN A KAMPUNG GIRL A CITY GIRL.

minah : Hello, is that Iz. In Kuala Lumpur?

Iz : Yes, Is that minah speaking, from the kampung?

minah : How are you and your life now? Do you enjoy living in Kuala Lumpur?

Iz : Oh, I'm very well now. Of course I enjoy it very much. I have found a good job for me now and I can save some money for my future. How about you, have you found any job by now?

minah : Oh ...... not yet, I'm still looking for it until now. There are not to many jobs here, its hard to find one.

Iz : If you want, come on and join me. I will help you get a job. Do you have an examination cutificate?

minah : Oh yes, I have SPM curtifizate, but is grade two.

Iz : That's all right, you could come. I'll help you to find a job. If you come and join me, yo will meet a miden range of people with different kinds of habit.

minah : I want to go to Kuala Lumpur but I find it hard to leave my parents and my relatives because they are close friends and family. Here I can continue traditional entertainment life ....

Iz : In Kuala Lumpur you can keep good health because they are soo many doctors and more medical facilities.

minah : O.K. I'll join you in Kuala Lumpur. I will be there at 7.00 a.m at the bus station. next Sunday. Bye for now.

Iz : Bye. I'll be waiting for you.

Figure 6: Malaysia – dialogue between a kampong girl and a city girl.

would prefer to stay in the rural area when they leave school or move to a city to look for work.

The first piece is about agricultural production in Kedah (Figure 5). A pupil presents a personal view of her family's income, showing some of the realities of work and pay for the local rubber tapper, who supports a family of seven. Dollars flow from the rubber tree into the cup but the text shows that the small-scale farmer gets little of it. Her picture helps develop pupils' understanding of the relation between primary producers and export processes, and shows some of the effects of the international trade economy on family life in a developing country.

The second piece is an imaginary dialogue between a girl who has moved to the city for work and a girl who has chosen to stay in the kampong (home village) (Figure 6). This class task produced a lot of discussion and contrasting opinions among those who aspired to move to a city to seek a better life than their parents had. In this example, the rural girl rapidly changes her mind under her friend's persuasion and decides to go to Kuala Lumpur.

These pupil drawings were part of a Social Topic Exchange Materials (STEM) initiative between a secondary school in Malaysia where I was teaching in the mid-1980s and a school in North Yorkshire where a friend was teaching. The Malaysian pupils express their ideas in English, so making exchanges of ideas and learning easier for British pupils – although, ideally, language should be no barrier to cross-frontier learning. English is widely taught in Malaysia, which was once a British colony.

When I later created resources for Save the Children's new Education Unit, the pupils' words and pictures were incorporated into a secondary Geography pack: *Frontiers: Change and Development in Malaysia and Thailand*. The Malaysian contributions are the product of their classroom English lessons, which included a learning exchange on the topic of homes with secondary pupils in Yorkshire.

Save the Children's field office in Bangkok asked a number of rural schools to produce comparable pictures. The Thai pupils' drawings were exchanged with selected images from rural Malaysia and Yorkshire. The pupils' work was developed in a chain process that originated in South East Asia, linked to Europe and then returned to another area of South East Asia. The primary aim was to exchange pictures and accounts by pupils on a defined topic. Then these would be brought together as a resource for use in the UK, where they would contribute to a debate within secondary Geography about the value of learning about the world directly from young people in their own countries rather than through adult interpretations. The handbook in the *Frontiers* pack provides supporting maps and statistical information about migration and production in Malaysia and Thailand.

Studying household economies helps pupils and teachers to think about children's economic well-being today. Comparing the ideas from two classmates presents different ways of looking at children's wealth issues in distant places. The rubber tree reveals the economic hardship which had not been immediately apparent, concealed as it is behind the facade of the family home. The dialogue adds understanding of rural poverty and why life in the cities may seem more attractive for young people.

Learning about poverty issues is sensitive. One constructive approach is to develop learning about poverty in a UK context and then compare this with poverty in other parts of the world. The ways of seeing richer and poorer countries tends to differ. Schools may be teaching about 'developing' or 'under developed' countries in general without having the resources to study family incomes and the ways children contribute to them. Teachers should be looking for children's perspectives on issues of wealth and economic security.

The right of children to enjoy and achieve

Another outcome of *Every Child Matters* is enjoying and achieving. This corresponds to many rights in the *Convention,* including the right for family care

> States Parties shall use their best efforts to ensure recognition of the principle that both parents have common responsibilities for the up-bringing and development of the child. Parents or, as the case may be, legal guardians, have the primary responsibility for the upbringing and development of the child. The best interests of the child will be their basic concern. (18.1)

Governments have responsibilities to provide assistance to parents and guardians through 'the development of institutions, facilities and services for the care of children' (18.2), whether at community or national level. Other relevant Articles include 28 for access to education and 31 for leisure and recreation.

Article 28 of the *Convention* states that children have rights to basic education. If these rights are indeed in place, consideration is required of the right to quality education as identified in Article 29. But not even a classroom can be guaranteed in some parts of the developing world. This can be contrasted with the economically richer world where there is enough money to improve the quality of education for every pupil.

None of the *Millennium Development Goals* specifically refer to children's success and achievement but this can be assumed as the aim of all of them. Recent developments in educational thinking provide ways of teaching directly about happiness. One of the *Millennium Development Goals* concerns access for all children to education at primary level; another is about getting more girls into schools. Article 28 of the *Convention* recognises 'the right of the child to education... on the basis of equal opportunity'. Article 29 provides for the quality of education which should include 'respect for human rights and fundamental freedoms'.

Figure 7: Peru – street play

The outcome 'to enjoy and achieve' focuses more than the *Human Rights Act* does on children's progress and development. Most of the world's children have some experience of formal schooling but there are many who do not because of their family's economic circumstances. As well as helping to bring about universal access to education through campaigning, teachers can celebrate the children who are in school around the world. But it is also good to celebrate achievements that are not gained through education. Inviting children to share their ideas about what they feel good about in their lives brings other experiences into classroom learning.

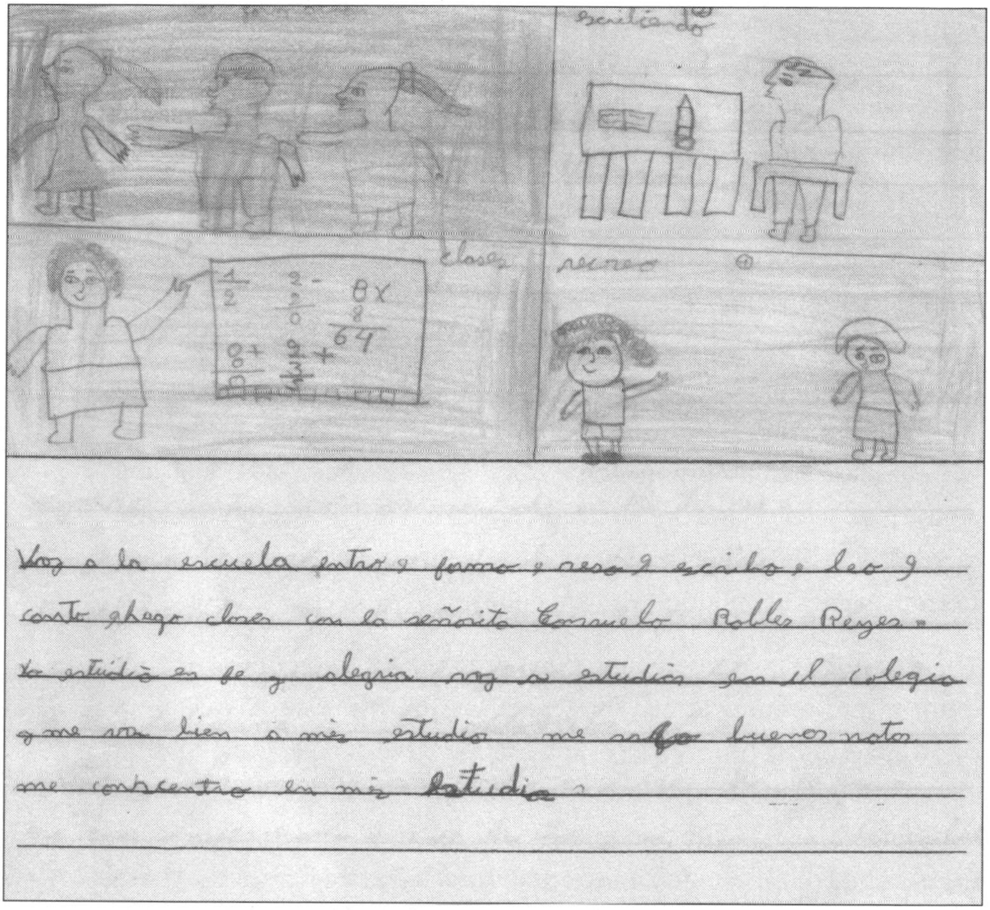

Figure 8: Peru – school scenes

My fifth scene is set in a primary classroom in an inner city area of Lima, Peru's spreading capital on the coast, in the early 1990s. I was shown around the area and met one family in their nearby home in a street which was still being built and which had brick water tanks outside each house. Because there was so much violence, I could not visit the school but the Brazilian photographer I was working with managed to do so. The local project workers arranged for exchange sheets from Bristol to reach the Lima pupils and for them to make their own project booklets on 'My life in the city'.

The first drawing by a primary age pupil in Peru's capital city shows his home area (Figure 7). The dry desert climate allows homes to have flat roofs, where clothes can be dried. Children are skipping and playing with spinning tops on the street between the houses and the traffic. The sun shines down.

The second drawing from Lima shows activities at school including outdoor learning and play as well as classroom writing and maths (Figure 8). The pupil who wrote about her drawings revealed her ambition to go on to secondary school. She was getting good marks and was conscientious about her studies. Many of the children I worked with in Lima had ambitions to be doctors or teachers. With a strong global media emphasis on the children who are not in schools because of poverty, civil conflicts or environmental disasters, it is good to learn from the views of children who are enjoying their lives at school.

The drawings on pages 28 and 29 are from NGO fieldwork with children in and around Lima. They were for the purpose of making a photo-pack for primary Geography, *Lima Lives* (Save the Children 1993). Although the output was one-way, the process entailed two-way communication. Primary pupils in Bristol made pictures of their homes and I took them to Lima to show pupils and their parents. These pictures acted like a passport, showing the kind of resource Save the Children intended to produce. This introduction was followed by an intensive two weeks of fieldwork in three working class settlements in Lima, in an attempt to present a little of the diversity of family histories, current lifestyles and actions for the future. Shorthand notes in translation were made about what the children said about their pictures. Thus the final publication was made up of factual inputs about city lives.

The drawings show a diversity of lifestyles in a crowded working class district of Lima. The El Agustino district has been settled by incoming families desperate for homes. They have taken over a steep hill close to the city centre and the central market which is a source of jobs. Their first houses may be no more than small temporary structures built from woven straw or cardboard but they stake a claim to land from which more permanent brick and plaster homes are developed. The residents then press the local council for water, sewage and electricity services or work co-operatively to provide them for themselves.

The El Agustino children shown in these pictures were happy to share images of their lives in the city with children in the UK. Save the Children initially hoped to produce a two-way resource based on stories from both Peru and England but funding would have had to come from the UK and this was not deemed to be a viable use of the NGO's money. However, the principle of enabling resources about children's daily lives in the UK and Europe to be developed for use in schools in other countries is worth highlighting. With collaborative support and financial backing, genuinely global resources could be produced that would give all children truer and more relevant knowledge than most traditional school resources about their peers elsewhere. There is more on this in section 2.3.

The right of children to safety

Children's rights can be improved by community, state and international action campaigns. Of particular concern is enabling children to learn about issues of access to education and about protection from the exploitative labour which harms children's progress to adulthood. 'Learning and labour' rights are considered in many of the articles of the UN *Convention*. Article 28 recognises that primary education at least should be compulsory and free to all (28.1). In addition:

> States Parties shall promote and encourage international co-operation in matters relating to education, in particular with a view to contributing to the elimination of ignorance and illiteracy throughout the world and facilitating access to scientific and technical knowledge and modern

teaching methods. In this regard, particular account shall be taken of the needs of developing countries. (28.3)

Children who are not in schools are exposed to harmful working conditions in order to add to family incomes. Article 32 of the UN *Convention* gives general protection against exploitation of children. Subsequent articles offer protection from drug abuse, sexual exploitation, trafficking and torture:

> States Parties recognise the right of the child to be protected from economic exploitation and from performing any work that is likely to be hazardous or to interfere with the child's education, or to be harmful to the child's health or physical, mental, spiritual, moral or social development. (32.1)

Being safe is another of the outcomes of *Every Child Matters*. This matches Article 19.1 of the *Convention*

> States Parties shall take all appropriate legislative, administrative, social and educational measures to protect the child from all forms of physical or mental violence, injury or abuse, neglect or negligent treatment, maltreatment or exploitation, including sexual abuse, while in the care of parent(s), legal guardian(s) or any other person who has the care of the child.

Another relevant Article is 39 for rehabilitative care.

None of the *Millennium Development Goals* are explicitly about child safety although in a way they all are. Environmental sustainability implies that environments should be kept safe for children to grow up in. A child's right to 'stay safe' at home and in the community is asserted in the *Human Rights Act*. All children share concerns and feelings for their own safety and that of others. Children may be equally in danger in rich countries and poor. Schools in the UK can celebrate examples of children who grow up safe and protected.

Figure 9: Panama – 'activities we do at home at different times of the week'.

Figure 10: Panama – 'the best people at providing for our needs'.

My sixth scene is set in a little two-class primary school in the Scottish highlands in the mid 1990s. The pupils are finishing their picture sheets showing aspects of their lives. They are to be exchanged with a class of the same age in rural Panama, Central America.

One of the images of daily life in Panama shows a child's daily activities in her community (Figure 9). The other is a child's view of who cares for her best (Figure 10). The first picture gives a strong visual representation of a child feeling safe in her community, helping at home, visiting the farm or walking to school. The second drawing shows a united family, a policeman helping children across the main road through the village and teachers all as caring adults. These pictures of carers for children at home and in the community help pupils and teachers to think about children's safety and who ensures it.

The focus of learning about the developing world is extended to aspects of caring for children and the children's own roles in their family and community. Such learning takes into account a broad spread of rights that include identity and cultural heritage. The essential right underpinning so much is the right to a family.

The *Caring and Sharing* project was designed to share children's ideas and experiences of childhood between schools in Scotland and Panama. There was an historical reason for this choice of countries: Scotland, then an independent nation, had briefly colonised the Atlantic coast of what became the state of Panama, through the Darien Scheme of the late 1660s. Contemporary maps of the coastline of Panama still show Scottish Point (*Punta Escoces*), illustrating how the past influences the present. There can be some validity in linking parts of the world that have already had links of a different kind.

For the project, Scottish and Panamanian children compared their views about who they think cares for them best. In Scotland the role of parents, baby sitters and Welfare State professionals was central. In Panama the dominant carers were the family, teachers, and the police on community service helping children across the road to school.

Two urban and two rural primary schools in each country were selected, and the work was directed at the top classes of eleven and twelve year olds. Worksheets were sent out to all four schools at the same time. They dealt with Caring for Children, Caring for the Environment and Sharing Resources. Each identified the area of enquiry at the top in English or Spanish, leaving the rest blank for the pupils' responses. Accompanying guidance for teachers suggested that responses should preferably be through visual illustration rather than writing, to overcome language barriers. Packages of the pupils' work then crossed the Atlantic by courier to the partner schools. Children in both countries were thrilled to receive direct responses to their own inputs, and the teachers in Panama evaluated the learning highly, as having given their pupils 'a window on the world'.

Other Save the Children projects have focused on children being compelled to work. This often prevents them from developing their full potential for learning and so may limit their future prospects. Child labour which restricts full development is a campaigning issue readily understandable by children who are in full-time education (see Resources for more information).

The right of children to health

Another outcome of *Every Child Matters* is being healthy. This matches Article 24 of the *Convention* which provides for 'the right of the child to the enjoyment of the highest attainable standard of health'. This Article points to the importance of health care and access to clean water and nutritious food. Other relevant Articles include Article 6 for children's rights to survival and development.

Three of the *Millennium Development Goals* are related to improving children's health. For all children to 'be healthy' is less of an issue than in the *Human Rights Act*. Media images and school textbooks often dwell on health issues in poorer countries. Although the disparities between rich countries and poor should not be denied, teachers should think about how they might provide a wider and more challenging picture of what is happening in the world and how children themselves perceive matters.

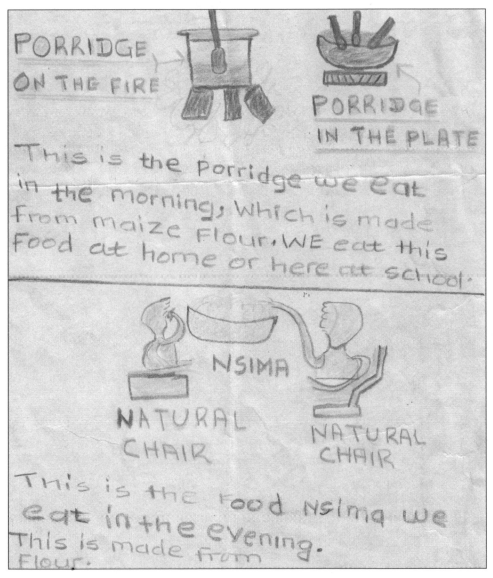

Figure 11: Malawi – 'food: what I eat in the morning and evening'.

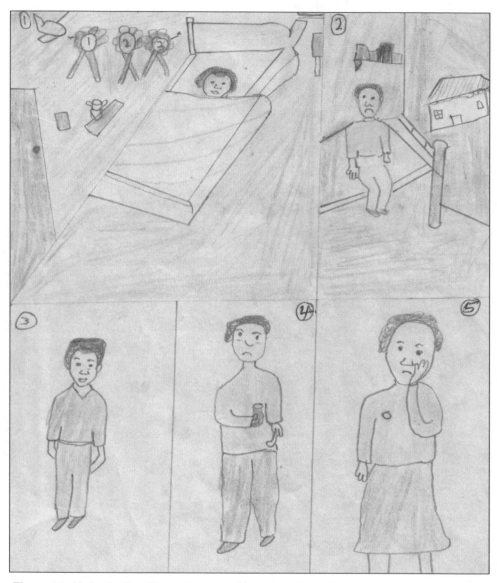

Figure 12: Malawi – 'health problems and how I got better'.

My seventh example is set in a primary school in Malawi in the late 1990s. I was on a fieldwork visit to an integrated health project supported by Save the Children, in a town near the Zambian frontier which had one secondary and several primary schools. I brought picture sheets and items from schools in Scotland to show the children aspects of their health, food, play, family and school life. The Malawian pupils were excited by these, regarding them as gifts which they wished to reciprocate. They were amazed at the wrappings of the box of cornflakes and contrasted it to how they grow and winnow their own maize around the school grounds. They also enjoyed their first experience of lego. They gave me handmade spinning tops, footballs and clay figures to take back to the Scottish schools.

The first picture shows maize porridge: the staple food of rural Malawi (Figure 11). The second drawing shows a child coming down with malaria and taking aspirin as a cure (Figure 12). These illustrate aspects of health relating to diet and medicine. Environmental and economic circumstances mean that a typical diet can satisfy a child's hunger without being very nutritious. A mother is shown providing health care for her child but lacking access to appropriate medicine – although aspirin may help alleviate the fever. However, the effective treatment of malaria entails prevention, for example sleeping under a net.

The right of children to participate

The last of the *Every Child Matters* outcomes is 'making a positive contribution'. This matches Article 29 of the *Convention* which provides for education to prepare the child 'for responsible life in a free society'. One of the newest areas of recognition of the rights of children in the *Convention* is for participation, expression and association. Other relevant Articles include Articles 2 for equality and 3 on seeking the best interests of the child. The whole *Convention* can be seen as giving children enhanced status in society.

Figure 13: Bristol – 'actions for the school'.

These pictures portraying how children contribute to their societies may encourage pupils in the UK to think about children's active participation in their society. One of the *Millennium Development Goals* is to build a global partnership for development. Young citizens should be brought into this partnership through learning to take appropriate action at local, national and global levels.

The notion of making a positive contribution is less evident in the UK *Human Rights Act*, even though this fits with current thinking about children being citizens in their own right. When learning about children in other countries, this concept may not be obvious, as ideas may be influenced by adult conceptions of development and progress. So it is important for teachers to look for examples of the various roles children play in family and local economies and as national and global citizens, and highlight them in the classroom.

Also relevant to the idea of children learning across frontiers are the illustrations of children's issues as seen by young refugees and asylum seekers. My eighth scene is set in a classroom in a secondary school in east Bristol during the early 2000s. The pupils were recently arrived refugees, mainly Somalis. It was difficult for these children to find school places in the city in the middle of the school year, but the Black Achievement Team at the school accepted children from newly arrived refugee and asylum seeking families.

Their task was to design drawings for the *Our School, Our World* class booklet. I worked with the pupils in a 'new arrivals' class pending their admission to mainstream classes, giving them a specially designed course in English language and Citizenship. Although the size of the group fluctuated there was a core of about fifteen, mostly girls and mainly from Kurdish and Somali backgrounds. Their ages ranged from 11 to 16.

The Somali girl's drawing here suggests actions that students could take at school to improve the toilets and also to raise awareness of

Figure 14: Somalia – 'Problems I have catching up with my learning'.
'Dhibaatooyinka aan wax la baran la'ahay'

racism (Figure 13). Her picture gives a sense of incoming children feeling safe and successful in their new school communities.

Our School, Our World encouraged the pupils' language skills and their understandings about Citizenship. The pupils created a publication that could be shared with others in the school and community and eventually be featured in a professional magazine for teaching Citizenship – which gave the pupils a powerful incentive. The final publication opened outwards from the pictures and ideas of the group, to the school, the city and the world. The language activities were designed so the pupils could put them onto picture sheets. This enabled every student in the group to work at their own level of awareness and linguistic capacity in English.

The class booklet was produced by young people who have direct experience of diversity and contrast in the world. The same techniques can be used to record the perceived similarities and differences between the known neighbourhood and the places the pupils are learning about. Picture sheets like these can then be shared between pupils in different schools and in different countries.

Comparing homes and family life styles in the examples discussed above show settled communities. This is true even in the case of the images from Lima of migrants who come to the city in search of better lives. Many children experience an unsettled childhood, especially those who are forced to leave their homes because of civil conflict. The resources listed at the end of the book feature images created by refugee children that relate to their welfare, safety and success and their contribution to their new host communities.

Figure 14 shows a desert area of Somalia where a group of children were asked by a Save the Children fieldworker to illustrate the difficulties they encountered in attending school regularly. I requested these drawings from Somalia while I was working at Save the Children's head office in London, so I could add the insights of children themselves to a role-play I was devising about education and participation for Early Years settings in England.

The drawing is of a boy standing on a rough platform scaring birds away from the family crops. He does so out of economic necessity but it prevents him from going to school. This can be taken as an example of participation, in which a child is contributing to family needs. It is also an example of poverty and of child labour. This reminds us how interconnected the elements are of learning about rights issues.

2.3: Classroom experience

This section offers teachers guidance on how to implement global learning in their classrooms. It suggests ways to benefit from cross-frontier exchanges, evaluate media presentations including classroom resources and develop imaginative activities which can lead to action for change.

Exchanging ideas

Encouraging pupils' rights to expression is directly related to promoting their sense of participation in school life and in the world beyond the school. Exchanges can be an effective way of developing learning across frontiers. The children share their ideas about common themes in their daily lives. Exchanges complement resources where there is scope for learning on both sides.

Structured learning exchanges are different from pen pal exchanges of letters or photographs. A sequence of activity based expressions can be developed. For example, in a Futures project for Year Seven English in an urban comprehensive school, the pupils wrote stories about the future and combined them with non-fiction descriptions of what would make a better future. The *Our School, Our World* project described above also illustrates how global learning can be structured into lessons. This project moved from capturing words and pictures for the class, the school and the community to personal accounts of the countries the refugee children had left.

The Malawi link described above demonstrated that exchange dialogues can be developed which follow the interests of the pupils. After the introductory exchange, pupils in one of the Scottish schools wanted to share ideas on the topic of water. So a second exchange of picture sheets was made. The right of children to expression was being realised, since it was they rather than the teachers who were guiding the direction of the exchange project.

Through exchanges of this kind children learn from and with other children across frontiers of nation state, language and culture. But such rewarding exchanges need careful planning and organising. Experience of establishing successful learning exchanges between schools in different countries indicates that good practice depends on certain factors

■ exchanges must be based on equality. The participants have to see it as an equal exchange, in which they can learn about differences and similarities by exploring a common theme or experience together

■ language should not be seen as an obstacle to exchanges across frontiers. Questions which encourage mainly visual responses are appropriate for younger pupils and should be translated into the first languages in advance

■ the children should share their views and the realities of their lives as this makes them feel valued

■ the resources selected should show realities of community lives, and particularly the roles of the children involved

■ open frame picture sheets with a question or topic heading at the top are ideal, and should be provided along with relevant information about the place concerned. This will provide a frame for pupils' responses. The rest of each sheet is blank, so each child or group of children can express their own realities through words or drawings on it. Drawings will be most useful where the exchange is between countries in which different languages are spoken.

The schools should complete their task so that the two lots of work-sheets can be exchanged at the same time. When they receive picture sheets from their exchange school the children already know the topics of enquiry and can readily respond to the visual images they receive from children growing up in a different physical, social and cultural environment. This facilitates comparison, so fostering their under-standing of issues of similarity and difference, be they in the games they play, family life or their experiences in school.

Teachers on both sides may need to sustain the motivation of their pupils by building up their anticipation of receiving more exchange material. Many exchanges have been set up in a flush of enthusiasm which soon fades on one side or both. This is not necessarily a total failure as some useful comparative learning will have taken place. However a realistic time scale for the project should be decided by the schools even before they begin.

The validity of the school linking being advocated by government departments and the *Times Educational Supplement* is currently under debate. One question is this: when does a learning or reciprocal exchange link turn into economic dependency? However, the examples of learning exchanges described in this book show how collaborative learning for global understanding can be initiated and sustained between school communities in different parts of the world that have very different levels of economic resource. In these projects, the pupils learned to see beyond definitions of 'development' based solely on narrow economic criteria.

These learning approaches are not exclusive to the NGO sector. I hope readers of this book feel inspired to create their own meaningful exchanges between young people and to learn from them. The key to success is that the purposes of the initiative should be agreed from the outset and that everyone involved should see the results.

These recommendations for improving global learning through exchanges all start from one vital principle: they are based on the genuine participation of the children – both those learning and those learned about. For children in the UK to become global citizens, they need to learn about the social, cultural, environmental, political, economic, spiritual and moral factors that drive the communities with whom they are learning. And they will need to learn how to relate their own lives to these aspects of the lives they are learning about in active and meaningful ways that transcend barriers of fundraising and empathy. Only then can children come to see a single world in which the lives of everyone impinge however indirectly, on the lives of everyone else so that action is possible for a common good.

Evaluating information

If pupils are to understand the similarities and differences between their lives and those of other children, sensitivity is needed. Photographs, films or textbooks used in schools often stress the differences, the exotic, the negative. Such images can be challenged by group tasks or class discussion. Begin, rather, by emphasising the positive and the similar. For younger children particularly it is good to start with a concept of common childhood, showing that all children play and most go to school. Pupils will then be better prepared to appreciate difference and begin to learn how histories, environments and traditions affect how children experience the world in different places. Examine the resources together and follow with group and whole class discussions about the images and the point of view of those who are presenting them.

This is certainly the way to approach topics on health and wealth issues in rich countries and poor. Such studies must be underpinned by the pupils understanding that all children have the same rights to grow up healthy and in economic security. Once this is established, pupils can explore the reasons why this is not true for all children and what might be done to enable them to access their rights as children.

That all children have rights to information highlights the importance of learning through contact with the real world rather than the one constructed by the writers of textbooks and classroom materials. The frontiers of children's learning will be extended by helping them to analyse the misrepresentations in their curriculum and materials and develop their critical thinking skills. It is important that they learn to put images of the world in context and explore why and by whom they were made. It is also important to encourage the participation of pupils in the provision of information. By learning to enquire and to express their ideas they are learning to explore the wider world (see final chapters for practical activities and resources).

Globalisation has created sophisticated means of communication which, if we ensure that children can access them, have the potential to increase understanding. It gives children the chance to make their own media to communicate in their own ways with other young people.

However, the mass media have huge impact on young people's attitudes towards the world they are growing up in. This influences their perception of others whose lives may be visible only through television or cinema screens. Studies of mass media images reveal the generally negative trends in reporting incidents in children's lives. The emphasis is on the sensational: shocking physical or emotional abuse of individual children or mass suffering because of war or disaster. Educators need to help young people deconstruct such messages and learn to look behind them. They need to ask questions about why and how the images were made and how much say the children portrayed had in the image-making process.

Everyone who is involved with children needs to treat images in this way. It can't wait for the teachers of Media Studies in secondary schools. Simply offering a range of visual contexts of urban and rural settlements in an African country may help stimulate thinking about the accuracy of the images. Pupils can take pictures of favourite places in their neighbourhood and add personal captions, then compare their images with pictures from other places, ideally through exchanging similar photo galleries with young people in other countries who have been given access to cameras.

The views of childhood in schools range from *concealed* childhoods, through *constructed* childhoods to *confided* childhoods.

Where children are rarely or never the subject of learning the childhoods are *concealed* or invisible. This is more likely to be the case at secondary school, when pupils move from the child-centred learning approaches of primary school. Courses in world history or citizenship include children in primary projects about, say, daily life in Benin or the Indus Valley but young people are seldom visible in the resources for twentieth century politics. Secondary lessons on the Second World War do indeed feature children evacuated from cities to country areas for their safety but this is merely the exception that proves the rule. As citizens, children have a right to be featured in lessons about all aspects of citizenship.

Flat, stereotypical or traditional presentations of children living in particular times or places, more like cardboard characters than living beings, are what can be termed *constructed* childhoods. 'Children of many lands' used to be a popular approach in primary Geography, with books showing children in colourful traditional costumes. Some rode camels; others picked tulips. National identities have their own truths or distortions in how they are represented. As well as the stereotyping, the children are portrayed as passive, posed and as taking no part in the active lives of their communities. This *National Geographic* or photographic view of difference fosters ideas of distance and strangeness between the children of the world.

The preferable approach is to present *confided* childhoods. The subjects of learning have had some say in how they are presented. Pupils are given images in which the children portrayed are shown as they want to be shown. This is not as difficult or complicated as it sounds. What it requires is for those who produce learning materials *about* children, be they commercial publishers or international development agencies, to ensure that they work *with* children in selecting and producing the images. Then the children learning from the resource will have a more richly fulfilling and honest experience than if some view of childhood has been filtered through remote adult hands. Producing resources on principles of confided childhoods will greatly improve how we learn from and with children about their own childhoods.

The resources for schools that development NGOs produce are best when they have been created through two-way learning processes across frontiers. But it may be impossible to show the lives of children in difficult social, economic and environmental circumstances in this way. And there are other restrictions on NGO educational activities in the UK: they are non government organisations, answerable to themselves, their constitutions and boards of management. Beyond these controls, most are registered as charities so come within UK charity law, and this places restrictions on activities which might be seen as politicised or indoctrinating.

Organisations like Oxfam and Christian Aid raise money and awareness in the UK to help alleviate the effects of poverty, conflicts and natural disasters in poorer parts of the world. The development agenda has meant that they have extended their programmes to support long-term development, although this has to be balanced against the needs for immediate relief. These organisations increasingly follow rights-based principles in developing their field programmes.

The UK-based development NGOs have established education departments that aim to raise awareness of their work for UK audiences. These are often called Development Education units. Although these may receive their funding by supporting the work of the NGO, the educational programmes are usually much wider. NGO development education workers collaborate across NGOs to help support learning in schools which they can base on their direct experience of programme work in developing countries. It can be difficult for teachers to tell whether the messages in an NGO resource have a fundraising or an educational purpose. However, resources of both types can be useful once their purpose is understood.

When doing fieldwork with children it is essential to communicate appropriately and to see things from the children's perspectives. A local researcher, community worker or adult is more likely to achieve this, as they are known and trusted by the children. The fieldworker also needs to be able to communicate directly with the children in their own language. Otherwise the information collected will be stilted and will not truly represent how they see their lives.

In the worst scenarios the information the fieldworker has provided is later altered to fit publishing requirements, and the final publication presents the expected negative image of children growing up in economically difficult circumstances. Thus to learn from children across frontiers demands not only their trust but also the producer's fidelity to what they say and express in their writing or drawing. Children brought into such fieldwork research processes should be clear about the purpose of the activity and how the information they give is going to be used. Ideally they should get to see the published outcomes of their expressions and be given a similar resource about children from the country where their own life stories will be used in the classroom.

When I was conducting fieldwork I found it useful to offer something of myself and my home background at the start. Even a simple colour postcard showing somewhere near where I live, with a personalised message of introduction or thanks written on the back, was well received. The final product and the learning that results will be made more meaningful if the subjects have been involved in selecting and captioning the images, and deciding how they would like their own realities to be presented to the learning community in another country.

The cover of this book indicates how resources can be collaboratively produced for use in schools in linked countries or all countries as a kind of shared book. Plan International has helped develop resources for use in a number of African countries as well as in the UK. Outside the NGO sector with its direct international contacts, LEAs have developed reciprocal learning links for social and civic learning, for example a learning link has been set up between Pembrokeshire in Wales and Zanzibar in Tanzania.

Teachers need to know the following about NGO resources:

- learning about children's rights and realities will be enhanced by using NGO learning resources. NGOs aim to promote good practice for developing materials and have produced an impressive range of resources on global childhoods for teachers and pupils.

- resource creation and dissemination can be improved through positive collaboration between teaching professionals and NGOs that are working directly with children and families in many – particularly economically poorer – parts of the world.

- giving a Globe Mark for authenticity to resources depicting childhood would help to improve teaching courses and learning resources.

A Globe Mark would be a kind of kite mark of educational standards for learning appropriately about the world. It is still only an idea but it might be developed by people who are reading this book. I would like to see some kind of validation developed by educators so that children can be assured of the usefulness and suitability of what they are being offered for learning about the world.

A new resource or project would only achieve a Globe Mark if it provided an authentic view of the experience it purports to represent. It would also be a guarantee that the people represented have had a say in the representation process.

It should be possible for commercial publishers and NGOs producing resources for global learning to meet and draw up an agreed code of practice for Globe Mark validation. If enough prestigious publishers could put their names to a standard mark of this kind, users would be better informed about the value of the resources they are downloading, buying and using.

It would certainly be good to see new or revised versions of learning resources for global childhoods receive a Globe Mark. Teachers will then no longer have to take the NGO on trust just because of its philanthropic reputation. They could tell at once that the resource has been approved by the children it is about. Perhaps we will move towards giving children and young people a voice in their learning which includes their being involved in the production of learning materials.

Imagining children's lives

Imaginative identification enriches fact-based learning about issues of change and community politics. Classroom activities that use role-play and drama are a powerful strategy for learning. Role-plays can help pupils to enter the daily realities of the lives of the children they are trying to help. They can also help to explore the potential and limitations of campaigning actions.

Role-play can be very effective in generating campaigns to improve the lives of children. The scenario should be authentic and open to being entered imaginatively. The children's own accounts of their ideas and experiences give the material authenticity. This was true of the role-plays on Burkina Faso and Somalia which I developed for Save the Children (see Chapter 5). The imaginative identification is helped if pupils understand about the similarities with their own lives. They will more readily put themselves in the situation of the people they are learning about and so better understand the differences in experience which restrict these children's lives.

Pupils can role-play a community meeting along the lines of what they know about local committee meetings, for instance. Imaginative identification is a path to commitment and campaigning activity and is likely to be much more effective than inviting responses to, say, a harrowing film of children in need. The role-play approach brings pupils closer to seeing the real children under consideration, who should be sharing the same rights as the pupils doing the role-play have themselves.

Drama-based learning methods like role-play and simulation are known to stimulate children's sense of involvement with the lives of other children, particularly those growing up in difficult or dangerous circumstances. The authenticity of dramatic scenarios which intro-duce child welfare issues in distant places is therefore vital. But learn-ing of this kind should not be weighed down by too many facts, as this could prevent children from identifying with the lives of others. The ultimate achievement of dramatic learning is its generation of cam-paigns on behalf of the children being learned about.

If teachers wish to foster campaign activities with their pupils, having them identify with the people concerned is the way to start. Resources and exchanges such as those described foster such identification. But too many resources about poverty and development fail to make the children featured vocal or visible, leaving the UK pupils feeling they are being asked to identify with adult communities. Learning exchanges may not be viable where the people most involved are not in school or have no access to communication resources such as computers and the Internet. Children in conflict situations might not want to communicate their personal views and experiences, even though knowing that children in other parts of the world are interested in them can be powerfully supportive.

School-based campaigning can evoke controversy. Pupils and their parents may perceive what the teachers initiate as being politically motivated and regard it as indoctrination rather than education. But the Citizenship agenda has raised awareness of legitimate areas of campaigning activity. Learning for social action is valued alongside learning for employment and academic achievement.

Children engage more readily in local campaigns than international or global ones. It is easier for them to survey local issues and express their ideas about them. There are many examples of pupil involvement with local councils, for example to make known their ideas about improving play facilities for children. Some councils have set up youth committees to facilitate such interactions.

Issues at national level become larger in scale and harder to influence. Writing to local MPs, inviting them into the school or arranging a visit to parliament are all valuable skills for political literacy. A class may study a national issue reported in the press and discuss their views on it. There must be opportunities for pupils to share their views more widely in the local community or the national press so their ideas do not go unnoticed.

However, pupils can be helped to feel empowered to make a difference globally. They can join supporter groups and receive information about campaigns like saving wildlife species that are threatened with extinction. They can express their opinions in writing and pictures which they communicate online. They can hold fundraising events for charities.

NGOs can support pupils and teachers with information and ideas for suitable activities. Older students might be able to work as volunteers in local or national NGO offices. They can contribute their skills either by directly supporting campaigning organisations or by organising their own campaigns.

Make Poverty History is a recent example of school-based campaigning. The campaign invited pupils to present their views at the G8 Summit in Scotland. A coalition of NGOs working under the banners of the Global Campaign for Education and Make Poverty History led the campaign. Pupils made and painted cut-out characters of their 'buddies' to show their concern for an imagined friend who could not attend school. The buddies were created from a downloadable template or designed by pupils themselves, then collected and taken to Scotland where they were displayed during the summit of world leaders. This campaign exemplifies how pupils can contribute their ideas to a common concern which is of global importance.

World AIDS Day, held on the December 1 each year, has an on-going global campaign in schools. A changing consortium of NGOs leads the campaign, using posters, badges and a creative website of classroom campaigning ideas. But the most successful global campaigning in schools has been for Red Nose Day. Inspired by Comic Relief, its combination of learning and action ideas has engaged children in helping to create a better world for the least well-off of the world's citizens. So if schools wish to develop global political awareness and capacity for action in their pupils they will find numerous sources of support.

There was once Empire Day, then Commonwealth and United Nations Days. Now Children's Day is celebrated each 20 November, to mark the date of the UN *Convention on the Rights of the Child*. Schools can obtain action calendars for assemblies or classroom activities. Special awareness days, like the global campaigns, motivate pupils to express their concerns about the state of the world and explore what actions they could take to improve matters. The number of worthwhile campaigns can make it difficult for teachers to cope with the pupils' choice of campaign. Pupils may feel moved to act on behalf of animals, the environment or economic injustices as well as issues which directly affect the opportunities and rights of children.

Multiple literacies

Active young global citizens require economic literacy. But they also need to develop political, social, environmental, emotional literacy as well as conventional literacy, particularly where the communities seeking to learn from and support each other do not speak the same languages. Guidelines are needed to help teachers achieve a common approach to this complex area of learning.

Active learning for global commitment should involve learning to take part in action at many levels. It is valid to learn global, act local, relearn global. Pupils who carry out a campaign to clean up the local environment can exchange what they have learned with pupils carrying out similar environmental activity in another part of the world. This enables all the pupils to see the world as a global community of which they are part. There can be many learning benefits from global exchanges. The pupils in the economically poorer world see that there are unsolved problems in a part of the world they have been led to see as richer and more successful than their own. Pupils in the richer world can see the power of action resting in the hands of young people in the supposedly poorer and more passive world beyond the familiar. If the pupils on each side of the exchange recognise that they have problems in common, they can learn ways of supporting each other to find mutually beneficial solutions.

Figure 15: Checklist for teachers to evaluate resources on global childhoods

Process

1. Who has produced this and why? Is the purpose made explicit?

2. When was this produced? How recent is it and will it be updated?

3. What role have children had in the production? What is acknowledged about the subject children or about children involved in trialling?

Content

4. What aspects of childhood are presented? Does the emphasis seem excessively positive, excessively negative or value-neutral?

5. What areas of the world are covered? How localised is this resource in accurate portrayals of family and community life?

6. How much visual or verbal evidence is there? Is there a real sense of these children's lives?

Method

7. What range of learning activities is provided? Is there a variety of learning approaches to 'distant' childhoods, including exploring media images and stereotypes?

8. How interactive are the learning activities? Does the resource offer creative ideas for classroom use or rely too much on a knowledge response or worksheet format?

Context

9. Is there scope to link with other relevant resources? Does the resource provide teachers with wider ideas, such as using links and school exchanges to learn more about children's lives?

10. What do you think about this resource? Is there an invitation to comment on and help improve the resource, for example by enclosing a return questionnaire?

Summary – interactive learning for children's rights

This chapter links the words of children and their pictures to their *learning* and *welfare* rights. These illustrate a variety of ways for increasing learning *about* children *from* children and show the diversity of art and presentation styles which children from different places and cultural backgrounds use when describing something of their lives and feelings. Much can be learned from their work

- The so-called poor world is rich in its potential for children to express themselves, and capacities to learn from one another. The possibilities can be explored through structured learning exchanges.

- Children can absorb complex values and understandings which challenge negative views of distant lives conveyed by the media and many textbook images. NGO resources are a source of corrective positive information about children's lives.

- Imaginative drama-based methods of learning are a way of developing understanding of the lives of other children and can lead to informed action like campaigning and support for charities.

- The comparisons made by young refugees and asylum seekers between the lives they had to leave behind and the lives they are making in the UK can be a source for learning about the world.

3
Crossing frontiers

Childhood as experienced by children around the world can and should be a valid source of learning in schools This chapter considers children's rights as a learning area in a holistic way, building on the specified outcomes of rights already described.

The movement for rights education in the UK is analysed and a forward-looking vision for classroom learning set out which gives importance to children's rights and to children learning about these rights in global contexts. Childhood is thus made a properly acknowledged source for school learning and this affirms children's rights to learn in its methodology and content. Such learning embraces the welfare rights of all the world's children.

Introducing understanding of children's rights can be merged with the practice of making children a subject in their own right of school learning. Curriculum reform on its own is not enough: also required is awareness of the need for improvement in the whole life of a school. Global childhoods cannot be taught about only within the constraints of fixed subjects. The entire school environment needs to respect the immediate rights of pupils to awareness and their own expression.

3.1: The movement for rights education

My ideas derive from my experience as a teacher working for NGOs and encouraging young people to express and share their ideas. The innovative approaches we used are part of a growing movement for education about, for and through rights which originates in the ideals of the United Nations for peace, tolerance and education 'regardless of frontiers'. It is supported by the UN *Convention* of 1989 and fits with peace education, development education, environmental education, multicultural education, antiracist education and global education.

The terms used in the fields overlap and can be confusing. The table below offers clarification.

EDUCATION – conceived and inspired by external organisations, e.g. UNESCO, NGOs	*International* education *Multicultural* education *Environmental* education	*Peace* education/ education for *peace* *Development* education/education for *development* *Citizenship* education/education for *citizenship*	*Values* education/ education in-for-through *values* *Human rights* education/education in-for-through *rights*
STUDIES – directed by and for teachers and curriculum needs	*Global* education	*Peace* studies *Development* studies *Citizenship* studies *World* studies	

Classifying these educational movements in this way emphasises that the purpose of human rights education is to enhance understanding of a plural set of values, as distinguished from movements aimed at achieving a single abstract entity like peace or development for all. Education about, for and through children's rights is a special subset of human rights education.

Following the Second World War, the United Nations agreed the *Universal Declaration of Human Rights* and set up UNESCO to promote international exchanges in education, and UNICEF to help care for children in greatest need.

UNESCO enabled the sharing of good educational practice across frontiers. An agreed set of *Recommendations on Education for International Understanding* (EIU) was drawn up in 1974. In the UK, the DES sought to influence educators, putting out a schools' circular in 1976 and setting up a Standing Conference on EIU in 1978. EIU is based on UN principles of peace and tolerance and aims to teach the next generation to understand countries and cultures outside the UK. 'International' is key concept, as much of the learning was about global politics and relations at country level. So EIU probably made most impact on upper secondary students, through courses in current affairs or external sixth form conferences.

From the start, UNICEF has worked to benefit children in need in the poorest countries. It has worked with governments to promote health care and education programmes, from which development education programmes have grown. UNICEF UK provides teachers with resources and training programmes for learning about children growing up in poverty.

Other approaches to learning globally and learning about children were also developed in the UK. In the late 20th century NGOs like Oxfam and Christian Aid helped to develop resources and resource centres for Development Education, which originated from a concern about poorer or less developed countries. Save the Children has a similar concern particularly with children. Amnesty International was created explicitly to focus on human rights. What the teaching world could see then and now is a diverse range of ideologies or educations from which teachers could choose approaches to world mindedness that they could develop with their pupils. From this wide-ranging field the term Global Education emerged as an umbrella for bringing all these educations together. Today the DCSF encourages a global dimension to school learning.

The shifts in the development of human rights education in the UK is illustrated below.

	Global/International	Peace/Development/ Citizenship	Values/Rights
1940s-1950s	UN/UNESCO	UNDP	UN UDHR (1948)
1960s-1970s	UNESCO *Education for International Understanding* (1974)	New Right criticism of *Peace* and *World Studies* UN Development Decades and growth of *Development Education* by NGOs, DECs and DEA	
1980s-1990s	Oxfam *Curriculum for Global Citizenship* (1997)	*Citizenship* as a theme in the England NC and Crick Report (1998)	*Values* in England NC. *Education in Human Rights Network*
2000s-	DfES/DfID support for *global dimension* in schools	QCA revision of KS3 *Citizenship*	DCA support for *human rights* in Citizenship at KS3

The strongest impetus for Human Rights Education followed the Second World War and the UN Charter's belief in avoiding peace and promoting respect for rights. The *Universal Declaration of Human Rights* (UDHR) appeared in 1948 and the terminologies and practices of education in human rights education were set down. These still inform the British and international movements. UNESCO promoted Education for International Understanding, emphasising the value of learning about human rights. During the 1960s and 1970s the independent Schools Council supported projects for integrated humanities and world studies, so developing learning approaches and materials for rights education.

In the following two decades an informal Education in Human Rights Network of NGO staff and teacher trainers met to produce guidelines and share ideas through a regular newsletter and annual conferences. Centres for the study of human rights were established in teacher training institutions, including the universities of Leeds, Leicester, London and Roehampton. Amnesty International, Oxfam, Save the Children and UNICEF, among others, published teachers' and class-room resources. Today many institutions are offering modules for Education Studies students on human rights education and related fields of development, environmental and global education.

The subject of children's rights still requires higher educational status but movement is in the right direction. The Qualifications and Curriculum Authority (QCA) offers a Key Stage Two unit for human and children's rights and the CITIZED website (www.citized.info) sets out specific guidance for children's rights learning in the early years. So there is progress. In 1998 George Flouris compared national educational curricula and found that there was far less on human rights in the UK than in France or Greece, and that in the UK there were 'no references to children's rights found in any of the subjects' (Flouris, 1998, 103). This is slowly being remedied. Education in the UK today allows for a new, lively and valuable movement for children's rights.

Human rights and wrongs are as old as human history; as old as the time people began making arrangements for how to live together in societies. Concepts of individual rights against governments grew during the revolutions in England (seventeenth century), America and France (eighteenth century) into the flourishing international human rights culture at the start of the twenty-first century. A key landmark was the creation of the United Nations after a world war ended in 1945 and the *Universal Declaration of Human Rights* (UDHR) in 1948. However the UDHR has been criticised as a formulation of western values, since the founder members of the UN who created it were primarily the victorious allied powers and the countries still under European colonisation had no voice in it (Freeman, 2002: 34-42; Pagden, 2003).

Nonetheless, the fundamental values enshrined in the UDHR – justice, peace, tolerance and respect – seem to have held up through more than fifty years of international tension. And the later United Nations agreements have more approval from the global community as the UN came to represent, albeit imperfectly, almost every world citizen. The UDHR does offer a minimum 'common standard' of values in an increasingly secular age, as expressed in its Preamble. The 1989 *Convention on the Rights of the Child* complemented the UDHR by clarifying rights for all children.

So human rights can shape a fundamental value system for creating viable educational policies. Implementing such policies in schools requires developing methods for young people to be learning about their rights and testing their social responsibilities. As universal values, human rights underlie courses in social and citizenship education, which should place greater emphasis on the specific area of children's rights.

3.2: Models for rights education

This section considers the case for making childhood and children's rights more centrally important in schools. It explores the potential in current subject areas for achieving a wide-ranging and forward-looking view of child rights education which emphasises the importance of children learning globally.

The increased interest in children's rights, especially participation rights, has created a climate for involving children more visibly and vocally in their social education, whether through personal and social education courses, the humanities or whole school initiatives. Since the UN *Convention* in 1989 a child-focused approach to subject learning has been growing in strength.

The *Convention* acknowledges children's education rights and also their participation rights, even if these are kept apart in the official text. The education articles (especially Article 29) provide teachers with a top-down recipe for teaching about peace, tolerance and justice issues today. This is compensated by the articles providing children with rights to expression (Article 12), to share information with others through any media of their choice (Article 13) and to have access to beneficial media information (Article 17). Teachers can focus on the subject matter of children and childhood as a rich source of exciting, motivating and child-friendly learning that can help to make issues come to life and have relevance in classrooms across age ranges and frontier divides.

Human rights education stresses that children should learn about all their rights. Before the *Convention*, children's rights were often regarded as something adults provided for children and a matter of protecting them. What is new about children's participation and expression rights is that children are now seen as active members of their communities and not just the passive recipients of adult support. There is scope to improve learning about specific childhood experiences worldwide and about the rights of all children. If rights of expression are not developed, pupils may receive an education in rights that is tokenistic, passive and adult controlled. But when expression rights are operating, children become active learners and members of their school communities. An emphasis on global childhoods broadens the picture, so that children come to understand their creative roles in their own societies.

The study of rights in childhood explores two main questions: 'what is life really like for children?' and 'how can pupils find out more?' The first question relates to perceived images of childhood and the ability to deconstruct them, for example when learning about a developing locality and viewing children in an African village setting toiling with buckets of water. The question challenges the image by prompting pupils to ask: how much does it show of the African child's real life? Who constructed the image? For what purpose? And what role did the children themselves have in deciding its final format?

The second main question follows: if pupils decide that there is more to be learned about these children and their communities than is shown by the resources, they should be encouraged to carry out further research. They might, for instance, interrogate the image makers in depth, perhaps inviting publishers or NGO education staff into the class. Or the range and depth of direct contact with the lives of the children being learned about is extended by scanning internet sources or seeking direct contact with the children in their own communities.

The most important thing is to not be bound by perceived frontiers of any kind in today's globalising world. In the past, as represented, say, in Thomas Hardy's novels of Wessex life, communication relied on hand-written notes – which were sometimes wrongly delivered. In today's world of globally connected communities it is possible to initiate exchanges via the internet, setting up e-mail dialogue, discussion groups or video conferencing. E-learning about children's lives should not be the only learning method, but experience of setting up cross-frontier learning initiatives on the internet has proved that they can be valuable experiences for everyone who takes part. When a 'global rights to expression' dimension is built into learning, it increases the scope for rights-based learning in schools. We live in a time when the possibilities for children's rights through global learning, regardless of frontiers, are constantly expanding.

The school can drive the learning about rights by means of its child protection policies and pastoral or personal education programmes or, alternatively, by its whole school and subject-led provisions for rights awareness. Ideally, the two approaches should work together. The former approach works outwards from the needs of individual children, the latter from the wider awareness inspired by the needs of children in difficult, rights-denying circumstances.

Some courses and resources have been constructed around what we can learn about children's daily lives in different countries, while others start from universal principles as enshrined in the *Convention*. The first approach is evident in, for example, the many secondary Geography lessons that focus on 'developing countries' and feature children – if they show them at all – as passive sufferers of poverty and exploitation who must be minders of younger siblings and carriers of firewood and water buckets. The latter approach connects with Personal, Social, Health and Citizenship Education lessons, in which pupils learn about the *Convention* and what their rights are. Many learning resources produced by development aid organisations seek to bridge the two approaches by relating issues of childhood poverty to the rights being denied to children. Such resources emphasise how children can help themselves and be helped by their families and communities, and by external aid, to gain these rights.

Such portrayals are clearly inadequate: much is missing about global childhoods. Focusing on the economically poor areas of the world tends to skew the subject matter of childhood too forcefully towards the negative. Some contextualisation of childhoods can be achieved when the learning is introduced through a photo-pack of, say, village life in India. But this may still provide pupils with only a narrow and inadequate view of childhoods in India today. Scaffolding children's learning by starting with portrayals of people's daily lives and moving them towards a grasp of abstract principles is complex. It is especially complicated for younger pupils, to whom it is not easy to explain why conceptually, a right is not the same as a need.

Writing on behalf of the Council of Europe, Hugh Starkey stressed the importance of trying to achieve more integrated models for human rights education in schools, especially secondary schools:

> The early years of education have a tradition of nurturing and caring. Post-primary education has often been a much harsher environment. Educators have increasingly come to realise the advantages of a caring and community-based approach to secondary education... Of course, a helpful school climate is not sufficient in itself to promote human rights education. There is a need... for 'a sequenced and meaningful' programme of study. Such a programme does not have to be based purely on knowledge. (Starkey 1991: 60)

For the youngest children, rights to survival, development, family care and health are fundamental. Logically these should be areas of rights that children learn about from the earliest years of formal schooling. A rights-based curriculum would look at how young children flourish and learn social values in a variety of settings. The Early Learning Goal for 'understanding the world' usually concentrates on child's immediate experience.

Bold colour maps and images broaden children's spatial understanding of the wider world. NGOs have produced innovative resources for this age level and details of some of them are given in the final chapter.

UNICEF's guide to *First Steps to Rights* offers teachers a broad range of child-centred learning ideas for introducing understanding of rights concepts with young pupils through, for example, using objects hidden in feely bags that relate to rights.

The Ragdoll Foundation/Save the Children produced a set of children's films from six countries called *What Makes Me Happy*. The films bring visual, aural and sense reality to the way children grow up, the ways in which they help in their own communities and how endlessly creative and inventive they are in using the simplest recycled resources.

During the middle years of schooling children can more readily identify global issues and their own potential role. At this age the rights to identity, information, expression and association become more meaningful in their lives. Two resources are particularly suitable for teachers to use at this stage:

Save the Children's *Young Lives, Global Goals* video resource pack supports an appropriately child-focused curriculum. In the video, children themselves speak directly to camera, describing some of the harsh realities of their lives as they grow up in conditions of poverty. There are eight interviews with children from four countries, allowing concepts of poverty and economic literacy to be understood through comparing the daily lives and prospects for a boy growing up in rural Ethiopia with, for instance, a girl growing up in the capital city, Addis Ababa.

Equally suitable is the primary teaching guide *Our World, Our Rights*, published by Amnesty International. It offers many useful activities based on a wide range of rights for teachers to use in class.

At upper secondary age the general provisions of the *Universal Declaration of Human Rights* become manageable. For adolescents it is appropriate to shift the emphasis to rights of protection from harmful labour, sexual abuse and exposure to drugs. NGO resources illustrate the effects of unfair trade on household economies in ways that are appropriate for secondary classrooms. This remit embraces personal, social and global views and provides at best an impressive array of wisdom from children in many parts of the world.

Global childhoods and universal rights are inter-connected and learning about them in schools is best done when they are addressed together. The chart overleaf suggests an appropriate integrated programme for pupils to learn about global childhoods and universal rights.

	Global childhoods	Universal rights
Early schooling (e.g. 3-7)	Positive comparisons e.g. laughing	Provision rights e.g. health, happiness
Middle schooling (e.g. 7-14)	Similarities and differences e.g. learning	Participation rights: e.g. expression, association
Late schooling (e.g. 14-19)	Negative comparisons e.g. labouring	Protection rights e.g. security, sexuality

This is inevitably simplified but the strands can be brought together through topic areas such as Celebrations, Futures or Child Labour. Because learning about rights must be developmental and progressive, so that children learn about the issues at their appropriate age, a checklist should be kept of their progress all through their schooling, to ensure breadth, balance, geographical spread and the possibilities for affirmative action.

A child-RICH curriculum

The learning strand of Rights in Childhood (RICH) can be incorporated in all schools and across frontiers. Focusing on RICH equips all pupils to become active, globally aware and concerned citizens who are learning to ensure their own rights and those of other children.

RICH is not a school curriculum subject that is taught to pupils by teachers. Learning will only be meaningful when educators and children actively co-operate. Child citizens who wish to present their own image will benefit from working in collaboration with skilled and experienced adult educators. Teachers should explore the possibilities for learning together and enabling children's expression about their childhoods.

When learning about global childhoods and children's rights in a sustained programme supported by dedicated resources such as those

Figure 16: A 'rich' curriculum

The following questions will be a stimulus for teachers and an aid to lesson planning.

1. **Rights**: *are courses based on rights principles?*
Is rights learning made explicit through studying rights documents? Or is it implicit in a set of principles underlying the course or lesson?

2. **International**: *is there a global dimension?*
Here the term international is an extension of the 'in' of Rights in Childhood. It comprises international learning in the exact sense of learning about interactions between countries and the cosmopolitan sense of accepting diversities of experience and viewpoints among people. Does it have specific global content or does it have a general dimension that looks outside the classroom and beyond visible frontiers of experience to inform learning?

3. **Children**: *Do children feature largely?*
How much are children a source of learning? Do pupils see pictures or hear voices of real children in courses and lessons? As well as a rights and a global dimension, is there an additional child dimension to school courses? Do schools teach about and through the experience of children?

4. **Childhood**: *Is childhood itself an area of study?*
The concept of childhood is a valid area of study in its own right – is childhood rather than adulthood a key area of school learning? Are the experiences of what it means to be a child in today's world central? Or is there an over-emphasis on the lives of individual and isolated children? Is meaning given to children's rights as a universal aspect of being a child?

described in this book, pupils encounter insights into the daily realities of childhood scenarios from around the world and they find them intriguing. At primary school they acquire a basic understanding of fairness and the rights that apply to all children. Scenes of playing and family life show them the positive aspects of children's lives in a variety of countries.

Once pupils have a basic understanding of the world's diverse interests and life styles they can connect more easily with, say, a disaster that suddenly strikes in some distant place on the world map. The event can be the subject of an assembly and in the classroom learning that follows the pupils can do internet research to learn more about the background and what happened. They learn about the event from a sustained global perspective. They find out what daily life was like for the local children before the disaster, and how matters could be improved. This approach gives scope for pupils to learn about the basic principles of international aid and development, and about ways of helping people to help themselves. Finally, they might consider what they might actively do about the situation, for example by raising funds in the school or local community.

With a firm foundation built at primary schools, pupils should continue learning about the world at secondary school. They are receptive to acquiring deeper understanding of why poverty is difficult to eradicate, why more boys than girls go to school in many countries and how environmental factors contribute to hunger and famines. Pupils who experience curriculum models of this kind will leave school as informed global citizens equipped to learn further about the world in collaboration with other young people and to take action for improvements they deem necessary and achievable.

Although *Every Child Matters* has identified five impact areas to make childhood better and ensure that all children in the United Kingdom get their rights, it does not go far enough in identifying childhood, and specifically global childhoods, as a source of learning. It is concerned with 'economic well-being' but does not link this to global learning or offer a global perspective.

The areas of government that are concerned with children and their education need to act in unison. While the DfES, now the DCSF, is advocating learning for citizenship, the DfID a more global approach with positive school linking and the Ministry of Justice more awareness of human rights in schools, there is no co-ordinated programme. A coherent set of guidelines is needed for children to learn about, from and with children.

Teachers need specific training if they are to teach children about children's issues on global lines and as informed by humans rights principles in the ways outlined in this book. Workshops for teachers on children's rights and responsibilities should be directly linked to child protection issues. Teachers and trainee teachers need to have a solid grasp of the global dimensions of childhood so they can compare the lives of children in other schools and communities with familiar rights contexts.

A book like this, focusing on learning about children's rights and realities with a global dimension, will, I hope, help to build up a valid learning area – but it is not a new school subject. If all new teachers were to follow courses in global childhood studies, the next generation of teachers will be far better equipped than the present one to teach children about children and to listen to children.

Summary – childhood as a source of learning

How children learn about the world beyond their immediate environment has engaged educators for many years. How can children in a community know and learn about children in other communities, particularly those distanced by space, time or culture? How do we help them overcome cultural distancing – the differences which have been

created between countries because of economic or democratic differences. This book is about how children in the so-called developed
countries can learn more truthfully and effectively from and about
children in the so-called developing countries. This is a two-way process. Another book is waiting to be written about how children in the
developing countries can learn from children in the developed countries.

Each time they plan or evaluate courses, teachers should ask these
questions:

■ Is there a global dimension to the course – does it entail learning beyond the locality and nation state?

■ Does the global dimension include learning about children –
are children's daily lives made visible, showing them with their
families and communities?

■ When children are presented, is it in light of their rights –
whether these are affirmed or denied – rather than as if they
are passive, silent, dependent on adults?

Bringing together aspects of human rights, children's views and global
perspectives in newly perceived and practised ways suggests a significant shift in teaching and learning. What matters most is that teachers
learn to listen to what children themselves express. We need to examine
how the voices of children from other places reach our classrooms and
how to ensure that communication is improved through encouraging
children to speak out for themselves. But this is seldom easy.

Children facing difficult economic or environmental circumstances
are unlikely to think that talking to a strange adult pointing a camera
and microphone is a priority. But once they understand that they are
being given an opportunity to speak and be listened to by the world
community who teach about their lives, they may see the potential it
offers for making changes to their circumstances.

When pupils and teachers in UK schools start to think along more global-local lines and set about trying to communicate with some of the children who live in the poorer parts of the world, they may understand their circumstances and develop the capacity to claim their rights more effectively. The *Millennium Development Goals* make it urgent for educators in the rich world to refocus their ideas through the lenses of childhood. When children are introduced to the concept of rights from an early age, as described in this book, courses in children's rights can be designed to fit across curriculum subjects and profoundly influence the schools' values and policies.

4

Practical guidance

This book takes a holistic approach to children's rights as a learning area, building on the specified outcomes in *Every Child Matters* for children's health, wealth, safety, celebration and contribution to society. It illustrates the ways in which childhood as experienced around the world today can be a valid source of learning in schools and how the most appropriate basis for such learning is the UN *Convention on the Rights of the Child.*

New approaches

For children themselves to be the subject of school learning the whole life of the school needs to change. The school environment has to respect the rights of pupils and affirm the positive messages being offered by the teachers. And the debate about how children's rights relate to their responsibilities has implications for how pupils conduct themselves in school.

In a survey by Birmingham University of ideas about citizenship for 7 to 11 year olds reported in the *Times Educational Supplement*, a Year 3 boy declared that 'children are citizens who do not get their rights met' (*TES*, 2/2/2007, p15). And a report by UNICEF in 2007 asserted that children in the UK are cared for less well than children anywhere else in the rich world. These surveys indicate that children need to learn at school that they are valued citizens with rights of their own.

The concerns discussed here cross the frontiers between the fields of human rights education, citizenship education and global education. Where the three meet, a new field is created: child rights education which is global in scope and which leads to positive action by young citizens. The NGO resources, which provide images of children in different parts of the world source the exploration of the new field. The book closes with accounts of activities and child-to-child projects for sharing views about the world and claiming rights to expression and to be heard, and gives details of the relevant publications.

The resources described feature the words and images from children in various countries. They are a rich stimulus for comparing childhoods in today's world. They can also act as longer-term sources for reflection on what children's participation could mean both for integrating the right of expression into schools and for extending this right to a truly global dimension.

> Through recognising children as citizens and engaging with student voices, educators, policy-makers and researchers can increase their understanding of learning and teaching processes and of what constitutes a successful learning community. Moreover, by drawing on the CRC as a framework they can ensure that the principles of inclusion and non-discrimination are built into their agendas. (Osler and Starkey, 2005: 39)

There is general international agreement that global citizenship education should be based on learning values for democracy, inclusion and human rights. But it seldom focuses specifically on the rights of children. This means that pupils will only be offered information and ideas which are based on adult conceptions and interpretations of democracy, inclusion and rights. And these are inappropriate for pupils who live in a global society that has signed up to the *Convention*. The task for educators is to incorporate children's own views of their lives so that their learning about global childhood rights and experiences is based on children's own understandings of reality.

Rights education teaches about universally accepted values. Participating in the world as global citizens entails sharing ideas about the world so that we come to understand other people, their ways of life and their values.

Pupils need to learn to see beyond the simplistic portrayal in the media and school materials of children's lives. This chapter outlines some activities to use in the classroom. They range from short discussion tasks to large-scale simulations and illustrate how resources which focus on children's lives in developing countries can be used constructively in the classroom. The examples that follow are drawn from various sources and can be adapted by teachers and pupils to suit their own learning.

Activities and approaches
Developing visual literacy
1. Integrating visual images

Photographs are powerful learning sources. They merit careful examination and discussion. Textbook images or class films are often afforded little more than a glance. Children will learn little from pictures they look at in this way. Stategies are needed for slowing things down so that they have to engage with the image.

The pupils need to work actively with the pictures they are given, rather than just looking at and discussing them. This can be done in several ways.

- The power of the captions could be explored

- The pupils to reflect on the pictures could write on the pictures.

- Or they could cut them up, then crop and caption them.

- Or the pupils could extend the focus of a picture by drawing what they think might be outside its frame.

We gave pupils photos which depicted children's lives in a range of contexts. They discovered that by attaching different sets of emotive words to them, the same pictures can be presented in either positive or negative light. This stimulated discussion about which images they think are accurate and representative.

When introducing the study of a particular locality, we need to start with a range of contrasting images of the place. Classes who make an imaginary journey to a chosen location might begin by presenting a travel agent's version of the country, featuring images of city hotels or beach resorts. They can then contrast this with a more realistic study of an African or Indian village.

2. Every Child Matters Everywhere

NGO development education units and the Geographical Association have produced locality packs for key stage Two Geography. The example illustrated here uses photographs of three children growing up in Lima, the capital city of Peru (Save the Children's photo-pack *Lima Lives* (out of print)).

The activity starts with a consideration of children's lives in the UK. The discussion is based on a simplified summary of *Every Child Matters* which relates the five outcomes to rights terminology as found in the *Convention*. The pupils can discuss the issues in groups or the discussion can take the form of role-play as an imagined family.

In the second stage, the pupils embark on an imaginative journey to investigate children's lives in another place. The discussion topic remains about rights, but in the new context. The discussion sheet is adapted to the different environment. The class should look at maps and photographs beforehand so they have a better idea of the reality of the place and the children who live there. Alternatively, photographs of different families can be given to the groups, as in the *Lima Lives* resource.

Finally, the pupils compare their thoughts about the two different countries, either in groups or as a whole class. In a role-play where the teacher is in role as an international child rights expert, the class can express their views in the form of a drama. In comparisons between the UK and Peru, for example, pupils quickly understand that the children in Peru are in need of material support for the decent housing and clean water that are their right. Infusing conventional learning about contrasting localities with issues of children's rights provides a common value base from which to compare the two countries. Without such a base there is a danger that rich world and poor world localities are over-contrasted and the differences between them amplified.

Developing emotional literacy

Fluent verbal and visual expression contributes to children's development of emotional literacy. In language and literacy lessons, pupils can be encouraged to express personal and global values. Knowing that their communications – be it a drawing, a piece of prose or a poem – will be read by other people besides the teacher is likely to motivate pupils to do their best. They will be far more engaged when they see that their letter is not going to be merely marked and returned but will be sent to a chosen destination and may well evoke a reply.

English offers scope for telling stories, learning from other cultures and expressing ideas, so it is ideal for increasing the range and quality of learning from children's experiences. Popular stories for children by such authors as J K Rowling, Jacqueline Wilson and Philip Pullman can be used to build up pupils' curiosity about the worlds of children's imagination and expression. Writing by children themselves that has reached publication, like the diaries of Anne Frank and Zlata, are also popular in schools. What is required is access to more such writings and for teachers of English to intensify the focus on children's own literary and artistic products.

Developing political literacy

Pupils use their imagination when they play games such as Christian Aid's *Trading Game*. It provides a microcosm of global economic inter-actions in which richer and poorer countries meet in the marketplace, so encouraging children to plan how they can act to help poorer countries.

3. High Seize

Other activities simulate global action campaigns to help pupils explore ways to set up and run their own campaigns. High Seize was developed during the 1990s as part of a European awareness campaign for young people about drugs and development. The simulation was run within the framework of regional youth parliaments convened to explore the global trade in drugs and aimed to influence European policy. It was designed to enhance the understanding of the youth delegates who later met with European parliamentarians in Strasbourg.

The setting for High Seize is an international conference on a ship in the Atlantic – hence the pun. Delegates from cocaine producing areas meet with traffickers, users and politicians in Europe. The scenario is intentionally implausible – a matter that is explored after the simulation is complete. At the simulated conference each party puts across its own perspective on the drugs issue and in inter-group discussions an attempt is made to reach some consensus.

This is a model for global campaigning which could be developed to focus on changing children's worlds, not only in relation to drugs policies but also more comprehensively. Pupils and teachers could use High Seize to devise campaign-based simulation models where children's parliaments in the rich world interact with those in the poor world in child-to-child political action. The simulation offers endless creative possibilities for pupils to explore.

Developing thinking about rights

This section describes classroom activities intended to help pupils explore their own rights values. They use group discussion activities which can stimulate thinking about aspects of children's rights. Simple to set up, the activities are models for promoting children's expression rights in the classroom and encouraging pupils to voice their opinions and share ideas.

4. Wants and needs cards

The UNICEF picture cards are designed to enable pupils to think about differences between wants, needs and rights. They are available in the *Time for Rights* pack (2003) or the basic idea can be adapted and the cards locally designed.

Some cards illustrate things which many people would rate as wants: an i-pod, a bicycle or a seaside holiday. Other cards illustrate basic needs like food, water, shelter and health care. A third set of cards illustrates rights concepts like justice, education, protection and participation. Because these are more abstract, they are harder to convey in a simple illustration. This is all part of the learning objectives and can be discussed after the activity is complete.

Pupils work in groups with the three sets of cards all mixed up. Their task is to sort them into three piles, agreeing which they think are wants, needs or rights. As they do so they should talk about what these words mean to them as individuals and as a group. When the task is complete, each group shares its decisions with the rest of the class and discusses the cards they found especially hard to place.

With the three key words written on the board, the class can determine what each means. Pupils generally decide that 'wants' describes things we would like to have but don't really need; that 'needs' are things that we have to have for life and development, but that 'rights' are more than basic survival and are also harder to define. If pupils have their needs and rights they will have a better life than if they have to live without them.

The cards can be used to help pupils learn that rights are given by society and that the rights of other people should be recognised. Responsibilities are necessary. So although the sorting activity is suitable for young children, the introduction of the concept of rights as universal values may be more readily understood by the older primary pupils. Also relevant is the wider learning context: the activity could be presented as an introduction to a topic on children's rights or it could be used for comparative learning about other children's lives.

5. Circles of rights

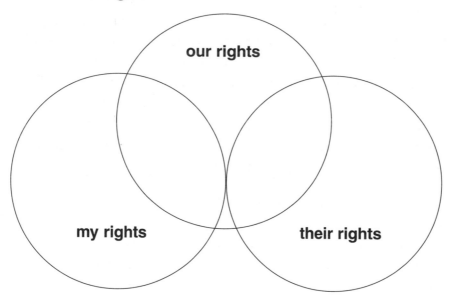

Draw overlapping rings and label them *my rights, their rights* and *our rights*. Discuss the implications of this model for building a coherent framework for children's rights education in schools. The left circle relates to how pupils learn about their own rights and related responsibilities, generally in PSHE or Citizenship. The right circle is about the denial or achievement of rights for children who are distant from them, as considered in humanities areas of learning, assemblies and fund-raising initiatives for international charities. The middle circle implies that pupils see their own rights and those of other children as related – although this may not be happening in a coherent way in their schools. The children's learning about their rights will only be fully achieved when all these connections are made.

Learning about 'my rights' – i.e. what official documents provide for my protection and development as a child – and about 'their rights' – i.e. how some children in the world do not have all their rights and why – should not be done separately. It is important that educators see and present 'our rights' and 'their rights' as connected. This is the only way that pupils can gain understanding about which groups of children are most at risk of lacking certain of their rights. Effectively connecting learning about the rights of children in the rich world and the poor develops pupils' skills of empathy and desire for action.

6. The Island Game

Amnesty International's Island Game is an activity for learning rights in the context of Citizenship. It provides a simulation model for pupils to think about universally agreed rights. Students space themselves around the classroom in groups of four to six. The scenario is that they have landed, in their groups, on a cluster of uninhabited islands after their plane crashed. In order to survive as a new society they will have to agree some principles for organising themselves and living together. Each group is given a large sheet of paper on which to draw up their charter of rights.

This simulation idea can be developed in many ways. When it is used to focus on ideas, each group presents its charter and these are discussed. But the Island Game can be extended by convening an inter-island meeting with the teacher in role as the UN Secretary General who has flown in. Still in simulation mode, each island can become aware of a neighbouring island and move to share ideas together. These larger groups can agree a general Magna Carta which incorporates the ideas in their own island charters. Whichever story-line is followed, the essential elements of this activity are to share ideas for basic rights principles for a good society, first in small groups and then as a whole class.

This should always be followed by an out-of-role discussion about what the pupils have learned from taking part in the activity. This may invoke explorations of what rights are, as well as the specific issue of whether the groups looked at democratic models for running their societies. Teacher facilitators may well find that they learn from running this activity with different groups in different learning contexts.

Another variation gives pupils relevant information at the outset about each person in the group, to prompt thinking about equality rights. For example, they might be told that each of them represents ten men and women, adults and children, able and disabled and so on. It all depends on what area of rights learning the activity is being used for: it can be a conceptual introduction or a detailed examination of certain rights.

5
Resources

Selected NGO resources relating to rights
Amnesty International: www.amnesty.org.uk

- *Human Rights in the Curriculum* (subject series: French, History, Mathematics, Spanish)

- *Learning about Human Rights through Citizenship* (secondary)

- *Our World, Our Rights* (primary: new edition forthcoming)

- *TeachRights teacher network*

Christian Aid: www.christian-aid.org.uk – Learn Zone

- *The trading game*

Council for Education in World Citizenship: www.cewc.org

- *Youth parliament on drugs and development* (final report)

Development Education Association: www.dea.org.uk

- *Human Rights: Guidance for Key Stages 2 and 3*

Oxfam: www.oxfam.org.uk/coolplanet

- *A curriculum for global citizenship*

- *Developing rights* (secondary)

- *Global Citizenship: The handbook for primary teaching*

- *Oxfam catalogue for schools* (annual)

Peace Child International: www.peacechild.org

- *Stand Up, Speak Out: a book about children's rights* (secondary)

Plan International: www.plan-uk.org – Plan-ed

- *Take your rights* (card game based on the *Convention*)

The Refugee Council: www.refugeecouncil.org.uk

- *Global Communities: Learning about Refugee Issues* (primary and secondary teaching resource)

UN: www.un.org

- *Teaching Human Rights: Practical activities for primary and secondary schools*

Unicef: www.unicef.org.uk – TeacherZone

- *Rights Respecting Schools* award scheme

- *Talking Rights, Taking Responsibility* (secondary)

- *Time for Rights* (primary and middle) with Save the Children

Save the Children resources relating to children's rights
Save the Children: www.savethechildren.org.uk/education

- *Citizens by right: Citizenship education in primary schools* (with Trentham Books)

- *Children's Rights: A Teacher's Guide* (ideas for teachers)

- *Eye to Eye* (photographs from refugee camps: www.savethechildren.org.uk/eyetoeye)

- *I've got them! You've got them!! We've all got them!!!* (booklets on children's rights and responsibilities)

- *One Day We Had To Run* (paintings from refugee children)

- *Partners in Rights* (art activities – see page 93)

- *Rights, Camera, Action* (for Media Studies) www.savethechildren.org.uk/mediastudies)

- *SCALES* (active learning examples – downloadable at www.savethechildren.org.uk/scales

- *What Makes Me Happy* (films inspired by children, with The Ragdoll Foundation – see page 92)

- *Young Lives, Global Goals* (child poverty and the Millennium Development Goals – see page 96)

The section below gives more detailed information about a selection of resources on children's rights produced by Save the Children. This is meant as a case study of how and why a certain NGO produces classroom resources for teachers.

For the early years
What Makes Me Happy – six films inspired by children in different countries

Available as a DVD, this set of films is the product of a creative partnership between Save the Children, which provided global reach, and the Ragdoll Foundation, which brought their expertise at entertaining and educating young children, as evident from their Teletubbies and Rosie and Jim television programmes. Save the Children set up workshops with teenage children in six countries to explore their memories of what had made them happy in their early childhood. With Ragdoll, scripts were created and young actors chosen to make the memories into films. The outcome is a collection of positive life slices in which children in places and circumstances that are usually portrayed negatively in the UK – such as Ethiopia and the Occupied Palestinian Territories (OPT) – paint, play and laugh together. In the film set in the OPT, Mahmoud is seen balancing his obligations to serve his local community through running errands against his longing to have time on his own to pursue his own ideas.

Teachers who have used these films have their favourites. One is the Sri Lankan story, filmed on location after the 2005 tsunami had devastated the coast. The film is about a girl, Hashi, who finds a damaged kite and – with the ingenuity and help of many other people – succeeds in repairing and flying it. This sense of fun in children's creative play is also evident in the film from Anhui Province in China, where Save the Children has a number of health and education programmes. Here, a boy, Junjie, uses scrap materials scavenged from the streets and people of the city to design his own toy.

These films use children's ideas to broaden global learning in the early years through relating to the similarities in children's experience. Children enjoy them because they see childhoods which are not too unlike their own. This suggests some parameters for effective global learning about childhoods. Both similarities and differences should be presented. Acceptance of similarities is the first step to appreciating differences. The dimension of happiness is vital – a major step forward for an NGO that exists to help children in the most difficult and damaging circumstances. But the difficult aspects of children's lives, particularly in the most distant and underdeveloped countries where Save the Children runs programmes, should not be disregarded. It seems vital to portray the good and the bad experiences in children's lives and not just the more common images of a terrible childhood.

Barriers to Learning role-play – access to schooling in Somalia

Somalia has been seriously affected by droughts and civil conflicts. Many families struggle to find basic food and water for survival. Although they regard education as very important it often has lower priority than migrating around the semi-desert land to feed families and livestock. Mobile teachers have traditionally provided some education for these nomadic families. Although schools provide greater resources as well as socialisation with other children and teachers, many families will not make the effort to send their children to school if it is hard to reach or evinces discrimination or if the toilets are inadequate. This is especially the case for the girls. Children in rural Somalia also responded to the specific questions on worksheets described in section 2.2).

The Somali children's drawings were used in primary schools in England to help trial a role-play activity for Early Years called Barriers to Learning. The children's pictures enriched the photographs of children's lives in Somalia. They helped the English pupils to identify with the children in Somalia. In a hot-seating activity the English pupils were invited to feel as if they were Somali children asking their parents – role-played by the teachers – to explain why they could not go to school.

This was followed by a role-play activity in which pupils in groups performed sketches to illustrate the obstacles to education faced by the Somali children, such as drought, hunger and poverty. The groups role-played families trying to work out how to overcome the obstacles. This active learning approach led the English pupils to identify strongly with the Somali children's lives and made them look for ways to help them get more schooling. They simulated action learning and planning campaigns. Fundraising activities and writing letters evoked eagerness to find out more.

This resource is available on-line from Save the Children as a downloadable role-play activity to help pupils enter the lives of these children imaginatively (www.savethechildren.org.uk/scales).

For the middle years
Partners in Rights – an arts-based pack on rights in the UK and Latin America

Funded by the National Lottery, the Partners in Rights project enabled a team of creative artists from Scotland to run arts workshops with children in Brazil, Cuba and Peru. Giant puppets were exchanged, and the participants made collages of what they saw as important in their lives. The outcome is a learning resource and website in three languages: English, Portuguese and Spanish. This ensures that everyone who was involved can see the results of their efforts and learning.

The artists led creative activities with children in the three Latin American countries. In Recife, Brazil, the project workers worked with groups of children in an Afro-Brazilian cultural centre, rather than in schools or family settings. They used a variety of arts techniques and gathered data from interviews in group sessions using interpreters. One child's response would set off others and soon a group would be conversing animatedly.

It is difficult to capture the children's spontaneity, and the nuances and complexity of the discussions when children talk things over together and with an adult from outside. And it is difficult to convert this rich experience into a printed resource. But it will inevitably be quite different to the typical formula of 'a day in the life of ...'. Instead of presenting one child the materials aim to provide a group or community portrait.

The best stimulus for sharing was to tell traditional tales. We chose a tale from Europe: *The Pied Piper of Hamelin*. Groups of children were encouraged to choose a tale from their continent and retell it by directing an adult artist to illustrate it. The point of this is to try and establish common areas of experience so that the outside adult researcher is drawn in and is no longer a stranger. This lively beginning generated spontaneous group conversations because the children understood what kind of insights into their lives were being sought and what information would be considered appropriate for the project.

Mining Minors – child labour in West Africa

This is a role-play, based on a project to combat child labour in West Africa. Children working in the gold mines in the north of Burkina Faso shared their experiences and voiced their concerns. Supported for many years by Save the Children, the project is now run by a local NGO.

Children do jobs in the local gold mine that are damaging to their health. Boys work underground in dangerous conditions to try and earn some money for their families in a part of the world where frequent drought conditions during the year make agricultural production virtually impossible. The boys bring rocks out of the mine and the girls work with their parents to sift through them in search of grains of gold. The children are working in family units, playing a role in their community. But they do so at the expense of their education and prospects in life. That children are out of school and in the workforce at a young age is recognised in richer countries as contravening the rights of children and instead education is compulsory.

The role-play based on this project allows the children to express opinions at a community meeting which would traditionally be dominated by adult male voices. Mining Minors was devised and trialled in UK primary schools. The role-play is set in a meeting that has been called to investigate children's working conditions and decide what can be done to stop or improve them. The participants represent different interest groups: elders, mine owners, parents, NGO workers and the children themselves. The elders' decision for the community prevails.

This resource is also available as a downloadable role-play activity at www.savethechildren.org.uk/scales

For older pupils and students
Young Lives, Global Goals – child poverty in four countries

The Young Lives Global Goals video pack shows the lives of certain children in Ethiopia, India, Peru and Vietnam and is designed for secondary Geography and Citizenship. It is based on a project for measuring and reducing poverty in families with very young children which was supported by the Department for International Development. The older siblings of the study children – who were all born in 2000 – feature on the video. This is about far more than holding up a camera to a child who is living in difficult economic and environmental circumstances. Teachers who use the videos appreciate the insights it offers into childhood worlds. It provides a realistic insider perspective for exploring with pupils the very topics that are often negatively treated topics in schools in the UK.

Brighter Futures – experiences of young refugees

Brighter Futures is designed to develop awareness of racism in host communities in three urban areas of England. Young asylum seekers and refugees meet regularly to share experiences, support each other and develop their communication skills. Brighter Futures groups have presented at national conferences. They maintain a website so they can spread awareness of the lives of young asylum seekers and refugees in the UK and some of the problems they encounter with immigration authorities and social services and the difficulty of gaining access to higher education. The visual montage is related to experiences of racist bullying that occurs in school and community settings and which also invade the privacy of mobile phones and personal computers. Such awareness raising demonstrates the positive contribution young refugees make through use of such media as the Brighter Futures website (www.brighterfutures.com).

At the time of writing, a role-play activity on *Rights against racism* is in progress. The Brighter Futures group of young asylum seekers and refugees in the north east of England is developing dramas based on the racist bullying they themselves have experienced. The idea is to use the specific examples of bullying in the classroom, around school, at leisure centres and through emails at home, and to re-enact them in various ways, for instance as a television reality show, where the simulated audience votes for appropriate strategies to tackle the bullying.

From beyond the UK

Save the Children's extensive educational programmes around the world have generated other valuable resources, such as the Listening to the Waters project in Cuba. Pupils made a study of flood patterns in their area, mapping out areas likely to be at risk. Then they set up an awareness raising programme for their parents, to show them how important it is to move to higher ground before the waters rise too high. There is a sense that the children are taking on community responsibility and educating their elders, recognising that their own rights to care and protection can be strengthened through action for the care and protection of everyone in the community (see scukcuba@enet.cu) with a booklet. Also available is a DVD: We are Prepared: Listening to the Waters).

Bibliography

Alderson P (2000) *Young Children's Rights: Exploring Beliefs, Principles and Practice.* London: Jessica Kingsley

Black M (1992) *A cause for our times: Oxfam, the first 50 years.* Oxford: Oxfam

Brown M and Harrison D (1998) 'Children's voices from different times and places', in Clough N and Holden C (eds) (1998) *Children as Citizens: Education for Participation.* London: Jessica Kingsley

Cunningham H (2006) *The Invention of Childhood.* London: BBC Books and BBC Audio Books

Eliot T S (1944) *Four Quartets.* London: Faber and Faber

Flouris G (1998) Human rights curricula in the formation of a European identity: the cases of Greece, England and France, *European Journal for Intercultural Studies*, 9 (1)

Freeman M (2002) *Human Rights: An interdisciplinary approach.* Cambridge: Polity Press

Freeman M (ed) (2004) *Children's Rights Vols 1 and 2.* Aldershot, Hants: Ashgate

Harrison D (2003) 'What are you going to teach asylum seekers about citizenship, Mr Blunkett?' *Teaching Citizenship* 5

Hicks D (2003) Thirty years of global education: a reminder of key principles and precedents, *Educational Review,* 55(3)

Lister I (1991) 'The challenge of human rights for education', in Starkey (ed) (1991) *The Challenge of Human Rights Education.* London: Casell

Osler A and Starkey H (eds) (2005) *Changing Citizenship: Democracy and Inclusion in Education.* Maidenhead: Open University Press

Pagden A (2003) Human rights, natural rights, and Europe's imperial legacy, *Political Theory,* 31(2)

Starkey H (ed) (1991) *The Challenge of Human Rights Education.* London: Casell

Times Educational Supplement. Democracy? I vote for Shilpa: Forget politics: citizenship for many pupils means fish and chips and 'Big Brother', February 2, 2007, page 15

UN (1989) *The United Nations Convention on the Rights of the Child.* New York: UN (referred to throughout this text as 'the Convention')

Index